Microwave
BAKING

Text by Judith Ferguson
Photography by Peter Barry
Designed by Philip Clucas
Produced by Ted Smart and David Gibbon

CLB 1676
© 1986 Illustrations and text: Colour Library Books Ltd.,
     Guildford, Surrey, England.
Text filmsetting by Focus Photoset Ltd., London, England.
Printed in Spain.
1986 edition published by Crescent Books,
     distributed by Crown Publishers, Inc.
ISBN 0 517 62735 3
h g f e d c b a

Microwave BAKING

CRESCENT BOOKS
NEW YORK

CONTENTS

Microwave baking will be a pleasant surprise if you love fresh-baked goods but not the long baking time. A single layer of cake will bake in 6-10 minutes, and a loaf of bread in 9-12 minutes.

At the start, the following points are worth remembering:

When baking in square or loaf dishes the mixture in the corners will cook more quickly than in the center. Wrapping the corners of the dish so that 2 inches of the mixture are protected will help prevent drying out.

Placing dishes on a rack or inverted saucer will allow heat to circulate underneath and help cook the bottom of cakes, bread or pastry evenly. Allowing the dish to stand on a flat surface for 5-10 minutes after baking will help the base to set.

Liquids do not evaporate as quickly in a microwave oven, so only add enough to bring the mixture to the proper consistency. When experimenting with conventional recipes, remember to cut down on the liquid.

Microwave ovens will cut the rising time for yeast dough almost in half. Place the prepared dough in a lightly-greased bowl large enough to allow the dough to double in bulk. Set the bowl in a shallow dish of hot water and cover tightly with plastic wrap. Microwave for one minute on MEDIUM setting and leave to stand for 15 minutes. Repeat the process until the dough has doubled in size. Loosen the covering as the dough grows.

Bread dough and other baked mixtures will not brown in a conventional microwave oven. Combination ovens, which use convection heat *and* microwave energy, will produce lightly-browned baked goods in about the same length of time as regular microwave ovens and they also give a crisper crust. But with such a variety of toppings, even conventionally microwaved cakes, breads and cookies can have an appealing finish.

Pastry baking has always been viewed as a microwave problem area. However, the edges of a pastry shell bake to a surprisingly crisp and flaky texture. Pre-baking a pastry shell unfilled is not recommended in a combination oven, but in a regular microwave oven it can produce a crisper base, as can the use of a rack or inverted saucer under the dish while baking. Leave the unfilled shell to cool on a flat surface for 5-10 minutes and the residual heat will help the bottom of the pastry to bake more evenly.

Microwave baking puts delicious desserts, cakes and pastries within easy reach. A microwave oven gives new meaning to that old cliché – the best thing since sliced bread!

Note: All recipes were tested in an oven with a maximum power of 700 watts and a combination oven with a maximum power of 600 watts.

YEAST BREADS

Honey Savarin with Strawberries

PREPARATION TIME: 1 hour

MICROWAVE COOKING TIME:
7 minutes plus 1 minute standing time

MAKES: 1 ring

⅔ cup milk
1 package active dry yeast
2 tsps sugar
⅔ cup butter
4 eggs
Pinch salt

SYRUP
½ cup honey
⅓ cup water
3 tbsps brandy

ACCOMPANIMENT
Whipped cream
Fruit

Heat the milk for 30 seconds on HIGH. Mix in the sugar and yeast. Sift the flour and salt into a large mixing bowl and warm for 15 seconds on HIGH. Make a well in the center of the flour and pour in the yeast mixture. Cover the yeast with a sprinkling of flour and leave until frothy, about 30 minutes. Stir together to form a batter. Soften the butter for 10 seconds on HIGH and add to the batter with the beaten eggs. Beat well for about 10 minutes by hand or machine. Butter a tube dish thoroughly and pour in the savarin batter. Cover the ring dish with greased plastic wrap and leave in a warm place 30-40 minutes. When the mixture has risen halfway up the sides of the dish, cook on

HIGH for 7 minutes. The savarin is done when the top looks dry. Leave to stand on a flat surface for 1 minute before turning out onto a rack. Place the honey and the water in a deep bowl and cook on HIGH for 7 minutes. Stir in the brandy and

This page: Cinnamon Fruit Braid. Facing page: Honey Savarin with Strawberries.

spoon the syrup over the cake to soak through. Serve with fresh fruit and cream.

Cinnamon Fruit Braid

PREPARATION TIME: 1-2 hours

MICROWAVE COOKING TIME:
8 minutes plus 5 minutes
standing time

MAKES: 1 loaf

BREAD DOUGH
2½-3 cups all-purpose flour
2 tbsps sugar
1 tsp salt
¼ cup butter or margarine
¼ cup water
½ cup milk
1 package active dry yeast
1 egg

FILLING
3 apples, peeled and roughly chopped
1 cup raisins
½ cup chopped candied citrus fruit
½ cup chopped dried apricots
½ cup brown sugar
¼ cup melted butter
¼ cup all-purpose flour
1 tbsp allspice

TOPPING
2 tbsps melted butter
1 tbsp sugar
1 tsp ground cinnamon

Sift the dry ingredients for the dough together into a large bowl and make a well in the center. Heat the water for 30 seconds on HIGH until warm to the touch. Stir in the yeast. Heat the milk and butter together for 30 seconds on HIGH and beat in the egg. Add to the yeast and pour into the well in the flour and gradually beat the liquid into the dry ingredients until well incorporated. Turn the dough out onto a lightly floured surface and knead about 10 minutes or until the dough is smooth and springs back when lightly touched. Form into a ball and put into a lightly greased bowl. Turn dough over to coat all sides. Cover the bowl with plastic wrap or a clean towel. Leave in a warm place for 1-1½ hours or until doubled in bulk. Alternatively, cover the bowl very loosely and set in a dish of hot water in the microwave oven at MEDIUM for 1 minute or on LOW for 4 minutes. Leave the dough to stand for 15 minutes. Repeat the process until the dough has doubled in bulk. This should cut the rising time almost in half. To shape the dough, punch it down and knead again, lightly, about 2 minutes. Roll out to a rectangle 8 inches x 10 inches. Cut the long edges at 1 inch intervals into 3 inch strips on the diagonal. Mix the filling ingredients together and mound down the center of the dough. Fold over the strips from alternating sides, down the length of the bread. Cover loosely with greased plastic wrap and leave to rise in a warm place for 30 minutes, or use the microwave rising method. Brush with the remaining melted butter, mix the sugar and cinnamon together and sprinkle over the top. Bake 6 minutes on MEDIUM, giving the baking sheet a quarter turn every minute. Increase the setting to HIGH and cook 1-2 minutes further, turning as before. The top should spring back when lightly touched if the bread is done. Leave on the baking sheet for 5 minutes before removing to a wire rack to cool.

Cinnamon Raisin Swirl

PREPARATION TIME: 1-2 hours

MICROWAVE COOKING TIME:
7-8 minutes plus 5 minutes
standing time

MAKES: 1 loaf

2½-3 cups all-purpose flour
2 tbsps sugar
1 tsp salt
¼ cup butter or margarine
¼ cup water
½ cup milk
1 package active dry yeast

FILLING
¾ cup flour
½ cup brown sugar
2 tbsps ground cinnamon
¼ cup butter or margarine
¾ cup raisins

TOPPING
2 tbsps butter or margarine, melted
1 tbsp cinnamon
¼ cup brown sugar

Prepare the dough as in the cheese and chive spiral loaf. Once the dough has been prepared and has risen to double in bulk, punch it down and knead it again lightly, about 2 minutes. Roll out to an 8 inch rectangle. Cut the butter for the filling into the flour and stir in the sugar and cinnamon. Add the raisins and scatter the filling evenly over the dough. Roll up from the long edge to the long edge. Seal the ends and tuck them under. Put into a lightly greased loaf dish, about 9 inch x 5 inch. Cover the dish loosely and leave in a warm place until doubled in bulk, about 30 minutes. Alternatively, follow the microwave rising method. Brush the top with melted butter. Mix together the topping ingredients and sprinkle over the bread. Cook on MEDIUM for 6 minutes. Increase the temperature to HIGH and cook 1-2 minutes. The top should spring back when lightly touched if the bread is done. Leave in the dish on a flat surface for 5 minutes before removing to a wire rack to cool.

Holiday Fruit Brioche

PREPARATION TIME: 1-2 hours

MICROWAVE COOKING TIME:
8-10 minutes

MAKES: 1 loaf

2½-3 cups all-purpose flour
2 tbsps sugar
1 tsp salt
¼ cup butter or margarine
¼ cup water
½ cup milk
1 package active dry yeast
1 cup candied fruit
⅓ cup chopped almonds
1 egg, beaten with a pinch of salt
Powdered sugar

Sift the dry ingredients together into a large bowl and make a well in the center. Heat the water for 1 minute on HIGH until warm to the touch. Stir in the yeast. Heat the milk and butter together for 30 seconds on HIGH and beat in the egg. Add the

Cinnamon Raisin Swirl (top) and Holiday Fruit Brioche (bottom).

mold. Form the remaining ⅓ of the dough into a smaller ball and put in the center of the dough in the brioche mold. Lightly flour the handle of a wooden spoon and stick the handle of the spoon through both balls of dough to stick them together. Cover the brioche mold with plastic wrap and set in a warm place for 30 minutes or until nearly doubled in bulk. The microwave rising method may be used as well. Brush the top of the brioche with the beaten egg and microwave on MEDIUM for 6 minutes. Increase the temperature to HIGH and cook for 1-2 minutes. If the dough still appears wet, cook an additional 2 minutes on HIGH. The top should spring back when lightly touched if the brioche is done. Leave in the dish for 5 minutes before removing to a wire rack to cool. Sprinkle with powdered sugar before serving.

Cheese and Chive Spiral Loaf

PREPARATION TIME: 1-2 hours
MICROWAVE COOKING TIME: 10 minutes
MAKES: 1 large loaf

3½-4 cups all-purpose flour
2 tbsps sugar
1 tsp salt
¼ cup water
½ cup milk
¼ cup butter or margarine
1 package active dry yeast

FILLING
½ cup grated Cheddar cheese
1 cup fresh breadcrumbs
3 tbsps chopped chives
¼ cup crushed cheese crackers
2 tbsps melted butter or margarine

Sift the dry ingredients into a large bowl and make a well in the center. Heat the water for 1 minute on HIGH until warm to the touch. Stir in the yeast. Heat the milk and butter together for 30 seconds on HIGH and beat in the egg. Add to the yeast

yeast and pour into the well in the center of the flour. Gradually beat the liquid into the dry ingredients until well incorporated. Add the almonds and the candied fruit and turn out onto a floured surface. Knead the dough for about 10 minutes, until the fruit and nuts are well mixed in and the dough is smooth and springs back when lightly touched. Form into a ball and put into a lightly greased bowl. Turn the dough over to coat all sides. Cover the bowl with plastic wrap or clean towel. Leave in a warm place for 1-1½ hours or until doubled in bulk. Alternatively, cover the bowl

loosely and set it in a dish of hot water in the microwave oven on MEDIUM for 1 minute or LOW for 4 minutes. Leave the dough to stand for 15 minutes. Repeat until the dough is doubled in bulk. This should cut the rising time almost in half. To shape the dough, punch it down and knead again lightly, about 2 minutes. Grease a brioche mold very well. Form ⅔ of the dough into a smooth ball and put into the oiled

5 inches. Cover and leave to rise until doubled in bulk, about 30 minutes, or follow the microwave rising method. Brush with butter and sprinkle on the crackers. Place dish on an inverted saucer or a rack. Cook on MEDIUM 6 minutes. Increase the setting to HIGH and cook 1-2 minutes. The top should spring back when lightly touched if the bread is done. Leave in the dish for 5 minutes before turning out onto a wire rack to cool.

Pâté en Brioche

PREPARATION TIME: 1-2 hours

MICROWAVE COOKING TIME: 8 minutes plus 5 minutes standing time

MAKES: 1 loaf

2½-3 cups all-purpose flour
2 tbsps sugar
1 tsp salt
¼ cup butter or margarine
¼ cup water
½ cup milk
1 package active dry yeast
1 egg

FILLING
1 can pâté

COATING
1 egg, beaten with a pinch of salt
Poppy seeds
Dry breadcrumbs

and pour into the well in the flour and gradually beat the liquid into the dry ingredients until well incorporated. Turn the dough out onto a lightly floured surface and knead about 10 minutes or until the dough is smooth and springs back when lightly touched. Form into a ball and put into a lightly greased bowl. Turn the dough over to coat all sides. Cover the bowl with plastic wrap or a clean towel. Leave in a warm place for 1-1½ hours or until doubled in bulk. Alternatively, cover the bowl very loosely and set it in a dish of hot water in the microwave

on MEDIUM for 1 minute or LOW for 4 minutes. Leave the dough to stand for 15 minutes. Repeat the process until the dough has doubled in bulk. This should cut the rising time in half. To shape the dough, punch it down and knead again, lightly, about 2 minutes. Roll out to an 8 inch rectangle. Mix together the filling ingredients and sprinkle over the surface. Roll up from the long edge to the long edge. Sprinkle a greased loaf dish with additional crushed crackers. Seal the ends and put, seam side down, into a prepared loaf dish, approximately 9 inches x

Sift the dry ingredients together into a large bowl and make a well in the center. Heat the water for 30 seconds on HIGH, until warm to the touch. Stir in the yeast. Heat the milk and butter together for 30 seconds on HIGH and beat in the egg. Add the yeast and pour into the well in the flour and gradually beat the liquid into the dry ingredients until well

This page: Caraway Rye Sticks (top) and Pumpernickel Rolls (bottom). Facing page: Pâté en Brioche (top) and Cheese and Chive Spiral Loaf (bottom).

incorporated. Turn the dough out onto a lightly floured surface and knead about 10 minutes or until the dough is smooth and springs back when lightly touched. Form into a ball and put into a lightly greased bowl. Turn the dough over to coat all sides. Cover the bowl with plastic wrap or a clean towel. Leave in a warm place for 1-1½ hours or until doubled in bulk. Alternatively, cover the bowl very loosely and set it in a dish of hot water in a microwave oven on MEDIUM for 1 minute, or 4 minutes on LOW. Leave the dough to stand for 15 minutes. Repeat until the dough has doubled in bulk. This should cut the rising time almost in half. To shape the dough punch it down and knead again, lightly, about 2 minutes. Roll out to a rectangle about 8 inches long. Place the pâté in the middle of the bread and roll the bread carefully around it. Tuck in the end and put the loaf seam side down into a lightly greased loaf pan, about 9 inch x 5 inch. Cover the dish with plastic wrap and set in a warm place for 30 minutes or until nearly doubled in bulk. The microwave rising method may also be used. Cook on MEDIUM for 6 minutes. Increase the temperature to HIGH and cook 1-2 minutes. The top should spring back when lightly touched if the bread is done. Leave in the dish 5 minutes before removing to a wire rack to cool. Slice and serve cold as an appetizer or for picnics.

Caraway Rye Sticks

PREPARATION TIME: 1-2 hours

MICROWAVE COOKING TIME: 6-8 minutes

MAKES: 16 rolls

3 cups rye flour
1 cup all-purpose flour
1 tsp salt
1 tsp brown sugar
1¼ cups milk
1 package active dry yeast
2 tbsps butter or margarine
2 tbsps caraway seeds

TOPPING
1 egg, beaten with a pinch of salt
Caraway seeds
Coarse salt

Sift the flours into a large bowl with the salt and make a well in the center. Add the caraway seeds. Heat the milk for 15 seconds on HIGH and stir in the yeast. Add the butter and the sugar and stir to dissolve. Pour into the dry ingredients and stir to incorporate. Turn out onto a floured surface and knead for 10 minutes. Shape the dough into a ball and put into a lightly greased bowl. Turn to coat all sides. Cover with plastic wrap or a clean towel and leave in a warm place 1-1½ hours, or until doubled in bulk. Alternatively, put the bowl into a dish of hot water and heat in the microwave oven for 1 minute on HIGH or 4 minutes on LOW. Leave the bowl to stand for 15 minutes. Repeat the process until the dough has doubled in bulk. To shape, turn the dough out onto a floured surface and knead again lightly, about 2 minutes. Divide the dough into 16 pieces. Shape into sticks, slightly thicker in the center. Place on lightly greased microwave baking sheets and cover loosely with greased plastic wrap. Leave in a warm place 30 minutes or until doubled in size. The microwave rising method may also be used. Brush each roll with the beaten egg and sprinkle with caraway seeds and salt. Microwave 3-4 minutes on HIGH per batch. Transfer the rolls to a wire rack and serve warm.

Whole-Wheat Loaf

PREPARATION TIME: 1-2 hours

MICROWAVE COOKING TIME: 10 minutes

MAKES: 1 loaf

3 cups whole-wheat flour
1 cup all-purpose flour
1 tsp salt
1¼ cups milk
1 package active dry yeast
2 tbsps butter or margarine
1 tsp brown sugar

TOPPING
1 egg, beaten with a pinch of salt
Bran

Sift the flours and the salt into a large bowl. Reserve half the bran from the whole-wheat flour and return the rest to the bowl and make a well in the center of the ingredients. Heat the milk for 15 seconds on HIGH. Melt the butter and dissolve the yeast. Stir in the sugar and pour into the well in the bowl and stir to gradually incorporate the ingredients. Turn out onto a floured surface and knead for 10 minutes. Put the dough into a lightly greased bowl and turn over to coat all sides. Cover with plastic wrap or clean towel. Leave to rise 1-1½ hours in a warm place. Alternatively, place in a dish of hot water and put into the microwave oven for 1 minute on HIGH, or 4 minutes on LOW. Leave the dough to stand for 15 minutes. Repeat until the dough has doubled in bulk. This should cut the rising time in half. To shape the dough, punch it down and knead again lightly, about 2 minutes. Roll out to a rectangle and then roll up tightly. Seal the ends and tuck under slightly. Put into a lightly greased loaf dish, about 9 inch x 5 inch. Cover the loaf dish lightly and leave to rise in a warm place for about 30 minutes, or use the microwave rising method. Brush the top of the loaf with lightly beaten egg and sprinkle on the remaining bran. Cook on MEDIUM for 6 minutes and give the dish a quarter turn every minute. Increase the temperature to HIGH and cook for 1-2 minutes, rotating as before. The top should spring back when lightly touched if the bread is done. Leave it in the dish for 5 minutes before removing to a wire rack to cool.

Facing page: Whole-Wheat Loaf (top) and Poppy Seed Braid (bottom).

Pumpernickel Rolls

PREPARATION TIME: 1-2 hours

MICROWAVE COOKING TIME:
6-8 minutes

MAKES: 16 rolls

3 cups dark rye or whole-wheat flour
1 cup all-purpose flour
1 package active dry yeast
1 tsp dill seed
1 tsp salt
¼ cup vegetable shortening
½ cup dark molasses
½ cup water
1 egg

TOPPING
¼ cup butter, melted
Sesame seeds

Sift the flours and salt into a large bowl. Heat the water for 30 seconds on HIGH and add the yeast. Stir in the shortening, molasses and egg. Pour into the dry ingredients and add the dill seeds. Stir well to incorporate all the ingredients. Turn out onto a floured surface and knead 10 minutes, until the dough is smooth and springs back when lightly touched. Form the dough into a ball and put into a lightly greased bowl. Turn to coat all sides. Cover with plastic wrap or a clean towel. Leave in a warm place to rise for 1-1½ hours or put the bowl into a dish of hot water in the microwave oven and heat on HIGH for 1 minute or on LOW for 4 minutes. Leave to stand for 15 minutes. Repeat the process until the dough has doubled in bulk. To shape the dough punch it down, turn it out of the bowl and knead, lightly, for 2 minutes. Divide into 16 pieces and shape into round rolls and knots. Place the rolls in a circle on microwave baking sheets. Cover loosely with greased plastic wrap and leave in a warm place for 30 minutes, or until the rolls have doubled in size. The microwave rising method may also be used. Melt the butter for 30 seconds on HIGH and brush over the surface of the rolls. Sprinkle on the sesame seeds and cook on HIGH for 3-4 minutes, turning the rolls over once during cooking. Cook in 2 batches. When the rolls are cooked, transfer to a cooling rack and serve warm.

Poppy Seed Braid

PREPARATION TIME: 1-2 hours

MICROWAVE COOKING TIME:
10 minutes

MAKES: 1 loaf

4 cups all-purpose flour
1 tsp salt
1¼ cups milk
1 tsp sugar
1 package active dry yeast
3 tbsps butter or margarine
1 egg, beaten with a pinch of salt
Poppy seeds

Sift the salt and the flour together into a large bowl and make a well in the center. Heat the milk for 1 minute on HIGH until warm to the touch. Stir in the sugar and the yeast. Add the butter and stir to melt. Pour into the well in the center of the flour and gradually beat the liquid into the dry ingredients until well incorporated. Turn the dough out onto a lightly floured surface and knead about 10 minutes or until the dough is smooth and springs back when lightly touched. Form it into a ball and put into lightly greased bowl. Turn the dough over to coat all sides. Cover the bowl with plastic wrap or clean towel. Leave in a warm place for 1-1½ hours or until doubled in bulk. Alternatively, cover the bowl very loosely and set in a dish of hot water in a microwave oven on MEDIUM for 1 minute or on LOW for 4 minutes. Leave the dough to stand for 15 minutes. Repeat until the dough has doubled in bulk. This should cut the rising time in half. To shape the dough, punch it down and knead again lightly, about 2 minutes. Divide the dough into thirds and roll each third into a sausage shape. Braid the thirds beginning in the middle and working out to the ends. Turn the ends under and place the dough on a microwave baking sheet. Cover very loosely and leave to rise about 30 minutes or use the microwave rising method. Brush with the egg and sprinkle over the poppy seeds. Cook 1 minute on HIGH. Lower the setting to LOW and cook for 9 minutes. The top of the bread should spring back when lightly touched if it is done. Leave the bread on a sheet for 5 minutes before removing to a wire rack to cool.

Coffee Almond Ring

PREPARATION TIME: 1-2 hours

MICROWAVE COOKING TIME:
8 minutes plus 5 minutes
standing time

MAKES: 1 ring

2½-3 cups all-purpose flour
2 tbsps sugar
1 tsp salt
¼ cup butter or margarine
¼ cup water
½ cup milk
1 package active dry yeast
1 egg

FILLING
1 can almond paste/2 packages ground
  almonds mixed with 1 egg white

FROSTING DECORATION
2 cups powdered sugar, sifted
Milk
Candied cherries
Angelica
Toasted almonds

Sift the dry ingredients together into a large bowl and make a well in the center. Heat the water for 30 seconds on HIGH until warm to the touch. Stir in the yeast. Heat the milk and butter together for 30 seconds on HIGH and beat in the egg. Add to the yeast and pour into the well in the flour and gradually beat the liquid into the dry ingredients until well incorporated. Turn the dough out onto a lightly floured surface and knead about 10 minutes or until the dough is smooth and springs back when lightly touched. Form into a ball and put into a lightly greased

Above: Coffee Almond Ring.

bowl. Turn the dough over to coat all sides. Cover the bowl with plastic wrap or a clean towel. Leave in a warm place for 1-1½ hours or until doubled in bulk. Alternatively, cover the bowl very loosely and set it in a dish of hot water in the microwave oven on MEDIUM for 1 minute, or on LOW for 4 minutes. Leave the dough to stand for 15 minutes. Repeat the process until the dough has doubled in bulk. This should cut the rising time almost in half. To shape the dough, punch it down and knead again, lightly, about 2 minutes. Roll out to a 12 inch rectangle. Spread with the almond paste. Roll up from the long edge to the long edge. Place the roll on a microwave baking sheet and form into a ring, sealing the ends together well. Cut at 2 inch intervals and turn each section on its side. Cover with lightly greased plastic wrap and leave in a warm place 30 minutes, until doubled in bulk. The microwave rising method may also be used. Brush with milk and cook for 6 minutes on MEDIUM. Increase the temperature to HIGH and cook 1-2 minutes, turning as before. The top of the ring should spring back when lightly touched if it is done. Leave on the baking sheet 5 minutes before removing to a wire rack to cool. Mix the powdered sugar with enough milk to make a thick but pourable frosting. Drizzle the frosting over the top of the ring and decorate with the cherries and angelica.

QUICK BREADS

Strawberry Shortcakes

PREPARATION TIME: 25 minutes

MICROWAVE COOKING TIME:
2-3½ minutes

SERVES: 6 people

1 cup all-purpose flour
Scant 1½ tsps baking powder
2 tbsps butter or margarine
⅓ cup milk
Salt
2 tbsps sugar

TOPPING
Ground browned almonds
2 tbsps butter

Sift the flour with a pinch of salt and
baking powder. Cut in the butter or
margarine until the mixture
resembles fine breadcrumbs and stir
in the sugar. This may be done in a
food processor. Add the milk and stir
or process just until the dough comes
together. Knead lightly and roll out
½ inch thick. Cut out rounds with a
3 inch cutter. Melt the remaining
butter 30 seconds on HIGH. Brush
the tops of each biscuit and sprinkle
on the ground browned almonds.
Microwave on HIGH for 2-5 minutes
until well risen. Turn the biscuits
every 1 minute to cook evenly.
Remove to a wire rack to cool. Split
and serve filled with strawberries and
whipped cream.

Baking Powder Biscuits

PREPARATION TIME: 15 minutes

MICROWAVE COOKING TIME:
2½-5½ minutes

MAKES: 8 or 9 biscuits

1 cup all-purpose flour
1½ tsps baking powder
2 tbsps butter or margarine
⅓ cup milk
Salt

TOPPING
2 tbsps butter
Dry breadcrumbs
Paprika

Sift the flour with a pinch of salt and
baking powder. Cut in the butter or
margarine until the mixture

This page: Strawberry Shortcakes.
Facing page: Fruit Scones (top)
and Baking Powder Biscuits
(bottom).

resembles fine breadcrumbs. This
may be done in a food processor.
Add the milk and stir or process just
until the dough comes together.
Knead lightly and roll out ½ inch
thick. Cut out rounds with a 2 inch
cutter. Melt butter 30 seconds on
HIGH. Place biscuits on a baking

mixture thoroughly. Fill into paper cups in a microwave muffin pan. Fill the cups half-full with the batter and sprinkle the ground browned almonds on top of each muffin. Microwave 3-5 minutes on HIGH. If the muffins still look moist in spots, they will dry out during standing.

Cornmeal and Bacon Muffins

PREPARATION TIME: 15 minutes

MICROWAVE COOKING TIME: 5-7 minutes

MAKES: 8-10 muffins

½ cup all-purpose flour
½ cup yellow cornmeal
6 strips bacon
1 small sweet red pepper, diced
1 tbsp sugar
2 tsps baking powder
¼ cup oil
1 egg, beaten
Salt
Paprika

Heat a browning dish for 5 minutes on HIGH. Add the oil and cook the bacon until crisp, about 2 minutes. Crumble the bacon and combine with the rest of the ingredients except the paprika. Mix well to blend thoroughly. Fill into paper cups in microwave muffin pans. Fill each cup half-full with the batter. Microwave for 3-5 minutes on HIGH. If the muffins still look moist in spots, they will dry during standing. Serve warm or allow to cool.

Apple Pecan Streusel Cake

PREPARATION TIME: 25 minutes

MICROWAVE COOKING TIME: 13 minutes plus 10 minutes standing time

MAKES: 1 cake

1½ cups all-purpose flour, sifted
¾ cup brown sugar
1 tsp baking powder

sheet. Brush the top of each biscuit with the butter and sprinkle on the crumbs and paprika. Microwave on HIGH for 2-5 minutes, until well risen. Turn the biscuits every 1 minute to cook evenly. Serve with butter or honey or thinly sliced country ham.

Honey Whole-Wheat Muffins

PREPARATION TIME: 15 minutes

MICROWAVE COOKING TIME: 7-9 minutes

MAKES: 8-10 muffins

1 cup whole-wheat flour
1½ tsps baking powder
Pinch ground ginger
Salt

This page: Apple Pecan Streusel Cake. Facing page: Honey Whole-Wheat Muffins (top) and Cornmeal and Bacon Muffins (bottom).

2 tbsps dark brown sugar
¼ cup honey
⅓ cup milk
¼ cup oil
1 egg, beaten
¼ cup chopped almonds

TOPPING
Ground browned almonds

Sift the flour with the baking powder, salt and ginger into a large bowl. Return the bran from the whole-wheat flour to the ingredients in the bowl. Stir in the brown sugar and add the honey, milk, oil and egg. Stir in the almonds and blend the

1 tsp nutmeg
1 tsp cinnamon
½ tsp baking soda
¾ cup milk with 1 tbsp lemon juice or
    vinegar
½ cup butter or margarine
1 egg, beaten

TOPPING
1 apple, peeled and thinly sliced
⅓ cup brown sugar
¼ cup all-purpose flour
½ cup coarsely chopped pecans
2 tbsps butter or margarine

Combine all the cake ingredients and mix for about 30 seconds, or until fairly smooth. Do not overbeat. Pour in an 8 inch round dish. Scatter over the apples. Do not put too many apples in the center. Melt the butter for the topping for 30 seconds on HIGH. Mix in the remaining topping ingredients and sprinkle over the apples and batter. Microwave 6 minutes on MEDIUM. Increase to HIGH and cook 6 minutes more. Leave to stand on a flat surface for 10 minutes before serving. Serve warm or allow to cool.

Fruit Scones

PREPARATION TIME: 15 minutes

MICROWAVE COOKING TIME:
3-4 minutes

MAKES: 6-8 scones

2 cups all-purpose flour
1 tbsp baking powder
¼ cup butter or margarine
2 tbsps sugar
¼ cup golden raisins
1 egg, beaten
¼ cup milk

GLAZE
1 egg white, lightly beaten
2 tbsps sugar
1 tbsp ground cinnamon

Sift the flour, salt and baking powder into a large bowl and cut in the butter or margarine until the mixture resembles fine breadcrumbs. This

may be done in a food processor. Add the sugar and the raisins and stir in by hand. Stir in the beaten egg and enough milk to form a soft dough. The dough should not be too sticky. Knead the dough lightly into a ball, then flatten by hand or with a rolling pin to about ½ inch thick. Cut into a 2 inch rounds or squares. Place the scones in a circle on a microwave baking-sheet and brush the tops with lightly beaten egg white. Combine the sugar and the cinnamon and sprinkle over the tops of each scone. Microwave on HIGH for 3-4 minutes, changing the position of the scones from time to time. Serve warm with cream or butter and jam.

Cheese and Dill Bread

PREPARATION TIME: 20 minutes

MICROWAVE COOKING TIME:
15 minutes plus 5-10 minutes
standing time

MAKES: 1 loaf

2 cups all-purpose flour
1½ tsps baking powder
½ tsp baking soda
2 tbsps chopped dill
2 tsps brown sugar
½ cup shredded Colby cheese
⅓ cup butter or margarine
⅔ cup milk with 1 tbsp lemon juice or
    vinegar
1 egg, beaten

TOPPING
2 tbsps dry breadcrumbs
2 tbsps grated Parmesan cheese
1 tbsp chopped dill

Combine the flour, baking powder, soda, salt and sugar in a food processor. Work in the butter and add the dill and grated cheese. Add the egg and milk. This can also be done with an electric mixer. Spread into a 9 inch x 5 inch loaf dish lined with wax paper. May also be baked in a round dish. Sprinkle over the topping and cover the edges of the dish with foil to cover the mixture 1 inch. This will prevent the edges of the bread drying out before it is

completely cooked. Microwave for 10 minutes on MEDIUM. Increase the setting to HIGH and cook a further 5 minutes. Remove the foil during the last 5 minutes of cooking. In a microwave-convection combination oven, cook on the highest temperature setting for 14 minutes. Leave the bread to stand on a flat surface for 5-10 minutes before removing from the dish to serve.

Whole-Wheat Soda Bread

PREPARATION TIME: 15 minutes

MICROWAVE COOKING TIME:
8 minutes plus 10 minutes
standing time

MAKES: 1 round loaf

2 cups whole-wheat flour
2 cups all-purpose flour
2 tsps baking soda
2 tsps cream of tartar
1oz butter or margarine
2 tsps brown sugar
1 cup milk with 1 tbsp vinegar or lemon
    juice

TOPPING
4 tbsps oatmeal

Sift the flours into a large bowl and return the bran to the bowl. Add the soda, cream of tartar and sugar. Rub in the butter until the mixture resembles fine breadcrumbs. This may be done in a food processor. Stir in the milk until the mixture forms a soft dough. Knead lightly until smooth. Shape into a round on a microwave baking sheet. Mark into 4 sections and sprinkle over the oats. Cook on MEDIUM 5 minutes. Cook on HIGH for 3 minutes. Leave to stand for 10 minutes on a flat surface and then cool on a wire rack before serving.

Facing page: Cheese and Dill Bread (top) and Whole-Wheat Soda Bread (bottom).

Hazelnut Date Bread

PREPARATION TIME: 20 minutes

MICROWAVE COOKING TIME: 15 minutes plus 5-10 minutes standing time

MAKES: 1 loaf

1½ cups whole-wheat flour
¾ cup brown sugar
1 tsp baking soda
1 egg, beaten
¾ cup water
1 cup dates, stoned and chopped
½ cup toasted, chopped hazelnuts

Combine the dates and water and heat for 5 minutes on HIGH. Leave to stand 5 minutes. Cream the butter and sugar together. Sift in the baking soda, flour and the pinch of salt. Add the dates and liquid along with the egg, beating until smooth. Stir in the nuts and spread into a 9 inch x 5 inch loaf dish lined with wax paper. Cover the ends of the dish with foil to cover the mixture 1 inch. This will prevent the mixture from drying out on the sides before the bread is completely cooked. Cook on MEDIUM for 10 minutes. Increase the setting to HIGH and cook for further 5 minutes. Remove the foil halfway through the last 5 minutes of cooking. In a microwave-convection combination oven, cook on the highest temperature setting for 14 minutes. Leave to stand on a flat surface for 5-10 minutes before removing from the dish to serve.

Pumpkin Raisin Bread

PREPARATION TIME: 20 minutes

MICROWAVE COOKING TIME: 15 minutes plus 5-10 minutes standing time

MAKES: 1 loaf

1 cup all-purpose flour
¾ cup sugar
1 tsp baking powder
1 tsp baking soda
1 tsp allspice
1 tsp ground cinnamon

1 tsp ground ginger
½ cup oil
2 eggs, beaten
¾ cup raisins
1 cup canned or cooked pumpkin

Sift the flour, salt, baking powder, soda and spices into a large bowl. Beat in the remaining ingredients, except the raisins, with an electric mixer for about 2 minutes. Stir in the raisins by hand and spread the mixture into a 9 inch x 5 inch loaf dish lined with a strip of wax paper. Cover the ends of the dish with foil to cover 1 inch of the mixture. This will prevent the mixture from drying out on the sides before the bread is completely cooked. Remove the foil after 5 minutes of cooking time.

This page: Pumpkin Raisin Bread (top) and Hazelnut Date Bread (bottom). Facing page: Cranberry Orange Bread.

Cook for 10 minutes on MEDIUM. Increase the temperature to HIGH and cook for a further 5 minutes. In a microwave-convection combination oven, cook on the highest temperature setting for 14 minutes. Leave to stand for 5-10 minutes on a flat surface before removing from the dish to serve.

Banana Coconut Bread

PREPARATION TIME: 20 minutes

MICROWAVE COOKING TIME:
17 minutes plus 5-10 minutes
standing time

MAKES: 1 loaf

2 bananas
1½ cups all-purpose flour
¾ cup sugar
½ cup plus 2 tbsps butter or margarine,
   well softened
2 eggs
⅓ cup milk
1 tbsp lemon juice
1 tsp baking soda
½ cup shredded coconut
½ cup chopped macadamia nuts
   (optional)

TOPPING
½ cup all-purpose flour
¼ cup dark brown sugar
2 tbsps butter or margarine

**This page: Banana Coconut Bread.
Facing page: Black Bottom Pie
(top) and Orange Hazelnut Pie
(bottom).**

Mash the bananas with an electric
mixer or in a food processor. Soften
the butter 5 seconds on HIGH and
add to the bananas. Sift in the flour
and the remaining bread ingredients
in the order given. Beat until well
blended, about 2 minutes. Line a
9 inch x 5 inch loaf dish with wax
paper and spread in the bread
mixture. Sprinkle over the topping
evenly and cover the ends of the dish
with foil to cover the mixture 1 inch.
This prevents the sides from drying
out before the bread is completely
cooked. Cook on MEDIUM for
about 10 minutes. Increase to HIGH
and cook for 5 minutes. Remove the
foil halfway through the last
5 minutes of cooking. In a microwave-
convection combination oven, cook
on the highest temperature setting
for 14 minutes. Leave to stand for
5-10 minutes on a flat surface before
removing from the dish to serve.

Cranberry Orange Bread

PREPARATION TIME: 20 minutes

MICROWAVE COOKING TIME:
15 minutes plus 5 minutes
standing time

MAKES: 1 loaf

1 cup cranberries, roughly chopped
Juice and rind of 1 orange
Water
½ cup sugar
⅓ cup butter or margarine
2 eggs, beaten
2 tsps baking powder
½ tsp baking soda
½ cup chopped Brazil nuts
¼ tsp ginger
1¼ cups all-purpose flour

Grate the rind from the orange and
set it aside. Squeeze the juice and
measure the amount. Add enough
water to make 1 cup liquid. Sift the
flour with the baking powder, soda,
salt and ginger. Cut in the butter or
margarine until the mixture
resembles fine breadcrumbs. Stir in
the sugar and add the beaten eggs,
orange juice and water, orange rind
and the cranberries. Mix until well
blended and pour into a 9 inch x
5 inch loaf dish lined with a strip of
wax paper. Wrap foil on the sides of
the dish to cover the batter 1 inch.
This will prevent the mixture drying
out before the bread is cooked.
Cook for 10 minutes on MEDIUM.
Remove the foil. Increase the setting
to HIGH and cook a further
5 minutes. In a microwave-convection
combination oven, cook on the
highest temperature setting for
14 minutes. Leave to stand on a flat
surface for 5-10 minutes before
removing from the dish to serve.

PIES & QUICHES

Orange Hazelnut Pie

PREPARATION TIME: 20 minutes

MICROWAVE COOKING TIME:
13-17 minutes

SERVES: 6-8 people

PASTRY
1 cup all-purpose flour
⅓ cup butter or margarine
2 tbsps shortening
¼ cup ground hazelnuts
2-4 tbsps cold water

FILLING
3 eggs
½ cup brown sugar
Grated rind of 1 orange
¼ cup orange juice
1 tbsp flour
Pinch of salt
1 cup roasted hazelnuts, roughly chopped

DECORATION
½ cup whipped cream
6-8 orange slices
Small sprigs of mint

Cut the butter or margarine and shortening into the flour with a pinch of salt until mixture resembles fine breadcrumbs. Add the nuts and enough liquid to bring the dry ingredients together into a ball. It may not be necessary to add all the water. This may be done by hand or in a food processor. Roll out to a circle at least 2 inches larger than the dish. Fit into a pie dish and crimp the edges if desired. Prick the base and sides well with a fork. Cook on HIGH for 5-7 minutes on an inverted saucer or a rack. If the pastry begins to develop brown spots, cover them with a piece of foil. If the pastry bubbles up, press it

gently back into place. Allow to cool slightly before filling. Mix all the filling ingredients together, except the nuts, with an electric mixer. Stir in the nuts by hand and cook about 3 minutes, stirring frequently. Pour into the pastry shell and cook on MEDIUM 8-10 minutes or until nearly set. The filling will set further as the pie cools. Serve with whipped cream and garnish with orange slices and sprigs of mint.
Note: If using a combination setting in a microwave-convection oven, use the highest temperature and bake the filling and pastry together for about 20 minutes. Do not pre-cook the filling or pre-bake the pastry.

Black Bottom Pie

PREPARATION TIME: 25 minutes plus chilling time

MICROWAVE COOKING TIME: 7½-13½ minutes

SERVES: 6-8 people

PASTRY
1 cup all-purpose flour
⅓ cup butter or margarine
2 tbsps shortening
Pinch of salt
½ cup toasted desiccated coconut
2-4 tbsps cold water

FILLING
1 tbsp gelatine
¼ cup water
2 cups milk
¾ cup sugar
1½ tbsps cornstarch
3 eggs, separated
1½ squares unsweetened cooking chocolate
½ tsp vanilla extract
1 tbsp rum
¼ cup sugar

DECORATION
Toasted coconut
Grated chocolate
½ cup whipped cream

Sift the flour with a pinch of salt. Cut the butter or margarine and shortening into the flour until the mixture resembles fine breadcrumbs.

Add the coconut and enough liquid to bring the dry ingredients together into a ball. It may not be necessary to add all the water. This may be done in a food processor or by hand. Roll out to a circle at least 2 inches larger than the dish. Fit into a pie dish or a removable base dish and crimp the edges if desired. Prick the base and the sides of the pastry well with a fork. Cook on HIGH 5-7 minutes. If the pastry begins to brown in spots, cover with a bit of foil. If the pastry bubbles up, press gently back into shape. Sprinkle the gelatine on top of the water in a small custard cup and leave to soak. Put the egg yolks, sugar and cornstarch together in a deep bowl and pour on the milk. Heat on medium for 2-4 minutes, stirring frequently until thickened. Melt the chocolate for 2 minutes on MEDIUM. Take 1 cup of the custard and mix it with the melted chocolate and vanilla. Pour into the pastry shell and smooth out. Leave to cool. Melt the gelatine for 30 seconds on HIGH and stir into the remaining custard along with the rum. Put into a bowl of ice water and stir constantly until beginning to thicken. Beat the egg whites until stiff but not dry and fold into the custard. Pour carefully on top of the chocolate layer and refrigerate until firm. Decorate with cream, coconut and chocolate.

Fresh Fruit Pizza

PREPARATION TIME: 25 minutes

MICROWAVE COOKING TIME: 6-9 minutes

SERVES: 8 people

PASTRY
1 cup all-purpose flour
⅓ cup butter or margarine
2 tbsps shortening
Pinch of salt
2 tbsps ground almonds
2-4 tbsps cold water

FILLING
2 cups ricotta cheese
1 cup semi-sweet chocolate, finely chopped

½ cup toasted almonds, finely chopped
2 tbsps honey
Milk or cream
2 kiwi fruits, peeled and sliced
1 cup strawberries, hulled and halved
2 peaches or tangerines

GLAZE
½ cup apricot jam, strained
Squeeze of lemon juice

Cut the butter or margarine and shortening into the flour with the pinch of salt until mixture resembles fine breadcrumbs. Add the almonds and enough of the liquid to bring the dry ingredients together into a ball. It may not be necessary to use all the water. This may be done by hand or in a food processor. Roll out to a circle at least 2 inches larger than the baking dish. Fit into a pie dish or a removable base dish and crimp the edges of the pastry if desired. Prick the base and the sides of the pastry well with a fork. Cook on HIGH for 5-7 minutes. If the pastry begins to develop brown spots, cover with a piece of foil. If the pastry bubbles up, press gently back into place. A removable base dish may be set on a rack to allow air to circulate underneath the pastry, or a pie dish may be placed on an inverted saucer. For the filling, mix the cheese, chocolate, almonds and honey together. Thin with milk or cream, if necessary, to bring to a spreading consistency. Spread evenly over the base of the cooled pastry. Put the jam and lemon juice into a deep bowl and heat on HIGH for 1-2 minutes. Thin with more juice or water if necessary. Peel and remove the pith from all of the tangerine segments or, if using peaches, peel and slice thinly. Arrange the fruit in circles on top of filling. Spoon or brush the glaze over the fruit, covering it evenly and filling in any spaces completely with more glaze. Cool to set before cutting to serve.

Facing page: Fresh Fruit Pizza.

Deep Dish Pizza

PREPARATION TIME: 25 minutes

MICROWAVE COOKING TIME:
19½-22½ minutes plus 5 minutes
standing time

SERVES: 6-8 people

PASTRY
1 cup all-purpose flour
⅓ cup butter or margarine
2 tbsps shortening
Pinch of salt
2 tbsps chopped mixed herbs
2-4 tbsps cold water

FILLING
2 tbsps oil
1 onion, chopped
1 clove garlic, chopped
1 green pepper, chopped
8oz mushrooms, sliced
8oz canned plum tomatoes
¼ cup tomato paste
*1 tsp each chopped basil, oregano and
    parsley*
Salt and pepper
1 small can anchovies, drained
1 cup shredded mozzarella cheese
¼ cup grated Parmesan cheese

Sift the flour with a pinch of salt.
Cut the butter or margarine and
shortening into the flour until the
mixture resembles fine breadcrumbs.
Add the chopped herbs. Add enough
liquid to bring the dry ingredients
together into a ball. It may not be
necessary to add all the water. This
may be done by hand or in a food
processor. Roll out a circle at least
2 inches larger than the baking dish.
Prick the base and sides well with a
fork. Cook on HIGH 5-7 minutes on
an inverted saucer or a rack. If the
pastry begins to brown in spots,
cover with bits of foil. If the pastry
begins to bubble up, press it gently
back into shape. Cook the onions,
green pepper, mushrooms and garlic
in oil for 30 seconds on HIGH in a
large bowl, loosely covered. Add the
tomatoes, paste, herbs, salt and
pepper and cook a further 4 minutes
on HIGH, uncovered, until reduced.
Pour into the pastry shell and top
with the anchovies and sprinkle with
cheeses. Cook 10 minutes on

**This page: Raspberry Soufflé Pie.
Facing page: Spinach and Bacon
Quiche (top) and Deep Dish Pizza
(bottom).**

MEDIUM on a rack or inverted
saucer. Leave to stand 5 minutes
before serving.

Spinach and Bacon Quiche

PREPARATION TIME: 25 minutes

MICROWAVE COOKING TIME:
17-19 minutes plus 5 minutes
standing time

SERVES: 6-8 people

PASTRY
1 cup all-purpose flour
⅓ cup butter or margarine
2 tbsps shortening
Pinch of salt
¼ cup ground walnuts
2-4 tbsps cold water

FILLING
6 strips bacon
1 shallot, finely chopped
8oz fresh spinach, well washed
4 eggs
½ cup light cream or milk
1 cup shredded cheese
Nutmeg
Salt and pepper

Sift the flour with a pinch of salt. Cut in the butter or margarine and shortening until the mixture resembles fine breadcrumbs. Add the walnuts and enough liquid to bring the dry ingredients together into a ball. It may not be necessary to add all the water. This may be done in a food processor or by hand. Roll out to a circle at least 2 inches larger than the dish. Fit into a pie dish or removable base dish and crimp the edges of the pastry if desired. Prick the base and sides well with a fork. Cook on HIGH for 5-7 minutes on an inverted saucer or rack. If the pastry begins to develop brown spots, cover with pieces of foil. If the pastry bubbles up, press gently back into place. Heat a browning dish for 5 minutes on HIGH. Cook the bacon 2 minutes per side. Drain and leave in strips. Cook the shallot in the bacon fat for 1 minute on HIGH and drain. Cook the spinach in 2 tbsps of water in a large bowl covered loosely with plastic wrap. Reserve 2 tbsps of the cheese for the top of the quiche. Mix the eggs, cream or milk, salt, pepper, nutmeg and remaining cheese. Drain the spinach well and chop finely. Add the spinach to the egg mixture and pour into the pastry. Arrange the strips of bacon on top like the spokes of a wheel. Sprinkle on the reserved cheese and cook on a rack or inverted saucer for 7-8 minutes until the filling is softly set in the middle. Leave to stand for 5 minutes before serving.

Note: If using a microwave-convection combination oven, choose the highest temperature setting. Fill the unbaked pastry with the filling and bake for about 21 minutes.

Sour Cream, Apple and Raisin Pie

PREPARATION TIME: 25 minutes

MICROWAVE COOKING TIME: 17-20 minutes

SERVES: 6-8 people

PASTRY
1 cup all-purpose flour
1 tbsp sugar
2 tsps ground cinnamon
⅓ cup butter or margarine
2 tbsps shortening
Pinch of salt
2-4 tbsps cold water

FILLING
3 eggs, separated
1 cup sour cream
2 tbsps flour
¼ cup sugar
Pinch cinnamon, clove, and nutmeg
1 cup raisins
2 small apples, peeled, cored and sliced thinly
½ cup milk

MERINGUE
3 egg whites
¾ cup brown sugar
¼ tsp cream of tartar

Sift the flour, sugar and the cinnamon with a pinch of salt. Cut in the butter or margarine and shortening until it resembles fine breadcrumbs. Add enough liquid to bring the dry ingredients together into a ball. It may not be necessary to add all the water. This may be done by hand or in a food processor. Roll out to a circle at least 2 inches larger than the dish. Fit into a pie dish and crimp the edges of the pastry if desired. Prick the base and the sides of the pastry well with a fork. Cook on HIGH for 5-7 minutes on an inverted saucer or a rack. If the pastry begins to brown in spots, cover them with a piece of foil. If the pastry bubbles up, press it gently back into place. Beat the sugar, egg yolks and flour together in a deep bowl. Add the spices, milk and sour cream. Cook on HIGH for 2 minutes and then stir. Add the raisins and continue cooking until thickened – about 6 minutes. Cover and set aside. Cook the apples 1-2 minutes on HIGH and add to the sour cream mixture. Stir well and spoon into the pastry. Spread to smooth out completely. Beat the whites and the cream of tartar until stiff but not dry. Gradually beat in the brown sugar until stiff peaks form. Spread over the filling to cover completely to the pastry edge. Cook on MEDIUM about 5 minutes or until the meringue is set. May be served slightly warm or cold.

Key-Lime Pie

PREPARATION TIME: 20 minutes

MICROWAVE COOKING TIME: 10-12 minutes

SERVES: 6-8 people

PASTRY
1 cup all-purpose flour
2 tbsps cocoa
1 tbsp sugar
⅓ cup butter or margarine
2 tbsps shortening
Pinch of salt
2-4 tbsps cold water

FILLING
1 can sweetened condensed milk
3 eggs, separated
¾ cup sugar
Grated rind and juice of 3 limes
1 drop yellow food coloring (optional)
1 drop green food coloring (optional)

DECORATION
Grated chocolate
Lime slices

Sift the flour with the pinch of salt, sugar and cocoa. Cut in the butter or margarine and the shortening until the mixture resembles fine breadcrumbs. Add enough liquid to bring the dry ingredients together into a ball. It may not be necessary to use all the water. This may be done by hand or in a food processor. Roll out to a circle at least 2 inches larger than the dish. Fit into a pie dish and crimp the edges of the pastry if desired. Prick the base and sides well with a fork. Cook on HIGH 5-7 minutes on an inverted saucer. If the pastry bubbles up, press gently back into place. For the filling, combine the egg yolks, milk, rind and juice of the limes and coloring. Beat until smooth. Pour into the baked pastry shell. Beat the egg whites until stiff but not dry. Beat in the sugar gradually until stiff peaks form. Beat in the cream of tartar. Spread the

Above: Sour Cream, Apple and Raisin Pie (top) and Key-Lime Pie (bottom).

meringue evenly over the lime filling out to the pastry edge. Cook on MEDIUM for 5 minutes or until the meringue sets. Allow to cool completely and then chill. Decorate with grated chocolate and lime slices before serving.

Raspberry Soufflé Pie

PREPARATION TIME: 25 minutes plus chilling time

MICROWAVE COOKING TIME: 5½-7½ minutes

SERVES: 6-8 people

PASTRY
1 cup all-purpose flour
⅓ cup butter or margarine
2 tbsps shortening
Pinch of salt
2-4 tbsps cold water
2 tsps instant coffee

FILLING
1 cup raspberries, fresh or frozen
¼ cup lemon juice and water, mixed
1 tbsp unflavored gelatine
¾ cup sugar
3 eggs, separated
1 cup whipped cream

DECORATION
6-8 whole raspberries
½ cup whipped cream

Sift the flour and the pinch of salt into a bowl and cut in the shortening and butter or margarine until the mixture resembles fine breadcrumbs. Mix the coffee and the water and add to the dry ingredients to bring them together into a ball. It may not be necessary to add all the water and coffee. This may be done in a food processor or by hand. Roll out to a circle at least 2 inches larger than the baking dish. Fit into a pie dish or a removable base dish. Crimp the edges if desired. Prick the base and the sides of the pastry well with a fork. Cook on HIGH 5-7 minutes. If the pastry begins to brown in spots, cover with a bit of foil. If the pastry bubbles up push gently back into place. To prepare the filling, purée the raspberries in a blender or food processor and sift to remove the seeds. Sprinkle the gelatine on top of the juice and water in a small custard cup. Leave to stand 5 minutes. Beat the egg yolks and sugar until thick and mousse-like. Fold in the raspberry purée. Melt the gelatine for 30 seconds on HIGH. Pour into the egg yolk mixture, stirring constantly. Put into a bowl of ice water and stir until starting to thicken. Beat the egg whites until stiff, but not dry. Allow the raspberry mixture to thicken until it begins to hold its shape. Then fold the egg whites into the raspberry mixture along with the cream and pour into the pie shell, mounding in the center. Refrigerate until firm. Decorate with rosettes of cream and whole raspberries.

Apple and Rose Petal Pie

PREPARATION TIME: 25 minutes

MICROWAVE COOKING TIME:
22-26 minutes

SERVES: 6-8 people

PASTRY
1 cup all-purpose flour
⅓ cup butter or margarine
2 tbsps shortening
Pinch of salt
2-4 tbsps cold water

FILLING
4-5 cups peeled, sliced apples
⅔ cup sugar
1 cup rose petals, washed and dried
2 tbsps flour
Pinch ginger

TOPPING
Pastry trimmings
1 tsp cinnamon
2 tsps sugar

Sift the flour and the pinch of salt into a bowl. Cut in the butter or margarine and shortening until the mixture resembles fine breadcrumbs. Add enough liquid to bring the dry ingredients together into a ball. It may not be necessary to add all the water. This may be done in a food processor or by hand. Roll out to a circle at least 2 inches larger than the baking dish. Fit into a pie dish or a removable base dish and crimp the edges of the pastry if desired. Prick the base and sides well with a fork. Cook on HIGH 5-7 minutes on a rack or an inverted saucer. If the pastry begins to brown in spots, cover with pieces of foil. If the pastry bubbles up, press gently back into place. Cut the pastry trimmings into circles or flower shapes. Prick lightly with a fork and sprinkle with cinnamon sugar. Cook 2-4 minutes on HIGH arranged in a circle on a microwave baking sheet covered with wax paper. Combine all the filling ingredients and put into the pastry shell. Cook 15 minutes on HIGH or until the apples are done. Top with the pastry cut-outs before serving.

Cherry Streusel Pie

PREPARATION TIME: 20 minutes

MICROWAVE COOKING TIME:
22 minutes

SERVES: 6-8 people

CINNAMON PASTRY
1 cup all-purpose flour
⅓ cup butter or margarine
Pinch of cinnamon
⅓ cup cold water
Pinch salt

This page: Apple and Rose Petal Pie (top) and Cherry Streusel Pie (bottom). Facing page: Corn and Tomato Quiche.

CHERRY FILLING
2 1lb cans pitted red cherries
¼ tsp almond extract
⅔ cup sugar
2 tbsps flour

STREUSEL TOPPING
½ cup all-purpose flour
3 tbsps butter or margarine

¼ cup chopped almonds
2 tbsps water

FROSTING
1 cup powdered sugar
2 tbsps water
Few drops almond extract

Sift the flour for the pastry with the cinnamon and a pinch of salt. Cut in the butter or margarine until the mixture resembles fine breadcrumbs. This may be done in a food processor. Add enough water to bring the ingredients together into a ball. Chill for 10 minutes and roll out to a circle at least 2 inches larger than the baking dish. Fit the pastry into an 8 inch pie dish and crimp the edges if desired. Place on a rack or inverted saucer. Prick the base well with a fork and cook for 5-7 minutes on HIGH. If the pastry bubbles up, press gently back into place. If brown spots appear, cover them with foil and continue baking. Mix the filling ingredients and pour into the pastry shell. Sift the flour for the topping and cut in the butter or margarine until the mixture resembles fine breadcrumbs. This may be done in a food processor. Stir in the almonds and add just enough water to make a crumbly mixture. Sprinkle the topping over the filling and cook a further 12 minutes on MEDIUM, or until the filling just begins to bubble. Sift the powdered sugar and beat in the water and almond extract. Add more water if necessary, but the frosting should not be too thin. Allow the pie to cool completely before drizzling over the frosting.

Corn and Tomato Quiche

PREPARATION TIME: 25 minutes
MICROWAVE COOKING TIME: 17-19 minutes plus 5 minutes standing time
SERVES: 6-8 people

PASTRY
1 cup whole-wheat flour
⅓ cup butter or margarine
2 tbsps shortening
Pinch of salt
2-4 tbsps cold water

FILLING
1 green pepper, diced
1 small onion, chopped
2 tsps oil
1 cup frozen corn, defrosted
4 eggs
½ cup light cream or milk
1 cup shredded cheese
1 tbsp chopped parsley
1 tbsp chopped dill
Salt and pepper
2 tomatoes, sliced in rounds

Sift the flour with a pinch of salt and return the bran to the bowl. Cut the butter or margarine and shortening into the flour until the mixture resembles fine breadcrumbs. Add enough liquid to bring the dry ingredients together into a ball. It may not be necessary to use all the water. This may be done in a food processor or by hand. Roll out to a circle at least 2 inches larger than the dish. Fit into a pie dish or a removable base dish and crimp the edges if desired. Prick the base and sides well with a fork and cook on HIGH 5-7 minutes on an inverted saucer or a rack. If the pastry begins to brown in spots, cover with pieces of foil. If the pastry bubbles up, press it gently back into place. Put the oil, pepper and onion into a small bowl. Cover loosely and cook 30 seconds on HIGH. Add the corn and cook a further 30 seconds. Combine with all the remaining ingredients except the tomatoes. Pour into the pastry shell and return the dish to a rack or inverted saucer. Cook 7 minutes on MEDIUM. Arrange the tomato slices on top and cook a further 5 minutes, until softly set in the middle. Leave to stand 5 minutes before serving. *Note:* If using a microwave-convection combination oven, choose the highest temperature setting. Fill the unbaked pastry with the filling and bake about 21 minutes.

Microwave
BAKING

COOKIES

½ cup roasted cashew nuts
Milk (as needed)

Beat together the butter and the sugar until light and fluffy. Add the egg, water and vanilla. Sift in the baking powder, salt and flour. Beat until just blended and stir in the nuts and the chocolate chips by hand. Add enough milk to bring to dropping consistency. Drop by rounded tsp amounts on wax paper in a circle of 6 cookies. Cook on MEDIUM 2-3 minutes per batch. Cookies may also be cooked in a microwave-convection combination oven for 3 minutes. When the tops look set the cookies are done. Remove on a paper and cool on a flat surface before serving.

Lemon-Iced Molasses Cookies

PREPARATION TIME: 20 minutes

MICROWAVE COOKING TIME:
12-18 minutes

MAKES: 48 cookies

½ cup butter or margarine
½ cup dark brown sugar
1 egg
2 tbsps molasses
2 tsps baking powder
2 cups whole-wheat flour
Pinch salt
1 tsp allspice
½ tsp ginger

This page: Chocolate Cherry Slices. Facing page: Lemon-Iced Molasses Cookies (top) and Chocolate Chip Cashew Cookies (bottom).

Chocolate Chip Cashew Cookies

PREPARATION TIME: 20 minutes

MICROWAVE COOKING TIME:
12-18 minutes

MAKES: 48 cookies

½ cup butter or margarine
½ cup light brown sugar
1 egg
1 tbsp water
2 tsps vanilla extract
Pinch salt
2 tbsps baking powder
2 cups all-purpose flour
1 cup chocolate chips

FROSTING
1lb powdered sugar
½ cup hot water
Yellow food coloring (optional)
Juice of 1 lemon
Rind of 1 lemon cut in thin strips

Beat the sugar and the butter together until light and fluffy. Beat in the egg gradually. Stir in the molasses and sift in the baking powder, flour, salt and spices. Stir together well and drop in 1 inch balls on wax paper on a microwave baking sheet. Arrange in a circle of 8 balls. Cook on MEDIUM for 2-3 minutes per batch, until the tops look set. Remove on a paper and cool on a flat surface. Prepare the frosting by mixing the powdered sugar and the hot water together. Add the lemon juice, strips of lemon rind and yellow food coloring, if using. Once the cookies are cool coat with the frosting and leave to set completely before serving.

Chocolate Peppernuts

PREPARATION TIME: 15 minutes

MICROWAVE COOKING TIME: 24-32 minutes

MAKES: 48 cookies

¼ cup butter or margarine
1 cup sugar
2 squares unsweetened chocolate
2 tsps baking powder
2 eggs
2 cups all-purpose flour
1 tsp black pepper
Pinch salt
Powdered sugar

Heat the butter and chocolate in a deep bowl on MEDIUM for 2-3 minutes. Beat in the sugar and eggs. Sift in the baking powder, salt, pepper and flour. Blend until well incorporated and chill until firm. Shape into 1 inch balls. Cook 6 at a time in a circle on waxed paper on a microwave baking sheet for 3 minutes on MEDIUM per batch. The cookies may also be cooked for 4 minutes on a combination setting of a microwave-convection oven. Cool

on a paper on a flat surface until firm. Sprinkle with powdered sugar before serving.

Rum-Raisin Cookies

PREPARATION TIME: 20 minutes

MICROWAVE COOKING TIME: 12-18 minutes

MAKES: 48 cookies

3 tbsps dark rum
1 cup raisins
½ cup butter or margarine
½ cup sugar
1 egg
2 tsps baking powder
2 cups all-purpose flour
Milk (as needed)
Pinch salt

Combine the rum and raisins in a small bowl. Cover loosely and heat 10 seconds on HIGH. Leave to soak. Beat the butter and sugar together until light. Beat in the egg gradually. Sift in the baking powder, flour and salt. Stir into the egg mixture until well mixed. Add the raisins and any remaining rum. If the mixture is very stiff, add some milk to bring to dropping consistency. Drop in a circle in rounded teaspoonfuls onto wax paper on a baking sheet. Cook on MEDIUM for 2-3 minutes or until the surface looks set. Cookies may also be cooked on a combination setting in a microwave-convection oven for 3 minutes. Remove the cookies on a paper to cool on a flat surface. Leave to cool completely before serving.

Chocolate Cherry Slices

PREPARATION TIME: 25 minutes

MICROWAVE COOKING TIME: 12 minutes

MAKES: 32 cookies

½ cup butter or margarine
1½ cups all-purpose flour
1 egg
½ cup powdered sugar
½ tsp cream of tartar

½ tsp baking soda
2oz unsweetened chocolate, melted
Pinch salt
48 candied cherries, halved
½ cup chopped, unblanched almonds
4oz semi-sweet chocolate

Melt the unsweetened chocolate 2 minutes on MEDIUM. Cool slightly. Beat all the ingredients together until a dough forms. Form into 4 sausage shapes about 1 inch thick. Press on 8 rows of 3 cherries and sprinkle over the almonds. Bake on sheets of wax paper on microwave baking sheets for 3 minutes on MEDIUM or until the top is set. Slice into 8 1 inch fingers while still slightly warm. Cool on paper or on a flat surface. Melt the semi-sweet chocolate for 2 minutes on MEDIUM. Drizzle over the cookies while the chocolate is still warm. Allow the chocolate to set completely before serving.

Walnut Fingers

PREPARATION TIME: 20 minutes

MICROWAVE COOKING TIME: 12 minutes

MAKES: 32 cookies

½ cup butter or margarine
1 egg
1½ cups all-purpose flour
½ cup powdered sugar
½ tsp cream of tartar
½ tsp baking soda
Pinch salt
½ cup ground walnuts
½ tsp vanilla extract
32 walnut halves
Powdered sugar

Beat the butter or margarine until soft, add the remaining ingredients except the ground walnuts and beat until a stiff dough forms. Stir in the nuts. Form into 4 long sausage shapes about 1 inch thick. Place on sheets of wax paper on microwave

Facing page: Rum-Raisin Cookies (top) and Chocolate Peppernuts (bottom).

baking sheets and flatten slightly. Push walnut halves down the center of each strip. Cook 2 strips at a time for 3 minutes on MEDIUM or until set on top. Slice into 1 inch fingers while still slightly warm. Cool on the paper or on a flat surface. Sprinkle with powdered sugar when cold.

Butter Pecan Bars

PREPARATION TIME: 25 minutes

MICROWAVE COOKING TIME: 12-13 minutes

MAKES: 12-16 bars

¾ cup whole-wheat flour
¼ cup butter or margarine
¼ cup brown sugar
2 eggs
⅓ cup plain yogurt
½ tsp baking powder
¼ tsp baking soda
Pinch salt
¼ cup chopped pecans

TOPPING
½ cup butter or margarine
1 cup dark brown sugar
½ cup chopped pecans
2 tbsps plain yogurt

Mix the butter and sugar together with an electric mixer until light and fluffy and add the eggs and remaining ingredients and beat about 1 minute. Stir in the nuts by hand. Spread into an 8 inch square dish. Cover the corners with foil and place on a rack or inverted saucer before baking. Cook for 6 minutes on HIGH. Remove the foil halfway through. Melt the butter for the topping for 1 minute on HIGH. Stir in the sugar and the nuts and cook for 3 minutes on HIGH. Add the yogurt. Spread the topping onto the bar mixture and cook on HIGH for 2-3 minutes until beginning to bubble. Cool and cut into bars.

Cranberry Bars

PREPARATION TIME: 15 minutes

MICROWAVE COOKING TIME: 10 minutes

MAKES: 12-16 bars

½ cup butter or margarine
⅔ cup brown sugar
1 cup instant oatmeal
1 cup all-purpose flour
Pinch salt
1 cup whole cranberry sauce
½ cup chopped walnuts

Beat together the butter or margarine and sugar until light and fluffy. Sift in

This page: Butter Pecan Bars (top) and Chocolate Chip Brownies (bottom). Facing page: Butterscotch Brownies (top) and Cranberry Bars (bottom).

the flour and salt. Add the oatmeal and blend until the mixture resembles coarse breadcrumbs. Press ⅔ of the mixture in the bottom of an 8 inch square baking dish. Put the dish onto a rack or inverted saucer. Cook on MEDIUM for 5 minutes or until just firm. Mix the cranberry sauce and walnuts together, and spread over the base. Crumble remaining oatmeal mixture over the

top and cook on HIGH for 5 minutes. Cut into squares while slightly warm. Allow to cool in the dish on a flat surface. Remove from the dish when cool.

Peanut Butter Thumb Print Cookies

PREPARATION TIME: 25 minutes

MICROWAVE COOKING TIME: 24 minutes

MAKES: 48 cookies

½ cup butter or margarine
1 cup smooth or crunchy peanut butter
1 cup light brown sugar
2 eggs
½ tsp baking soda
3 cups all-purpose flour
2 egg whites
1 cup coarsely chopped roasted peanuts
Grape or blackcurrant jelly
Redcurrant jelly or raspberry jam

Mix together the butter and the sugar until light and fluffy. Add the peanut butter and the eggs. Sift in the flour and the soda. Add a pinch of salt if using unsalted peanuts. Shape into 1 inch balls. Roll in lightly beaten egg white and then in the chopped roasted peanuts. Chill for 10 minutes. Press a well in the center of each cookie. Fill with 1 tsp jelly or jam. Arrange in a circle on wax paper. Cook for 4 minutes on MEDIUM. Cool on a flat surface before serving.

Chocolate Chip Brownies

PREPARATION TIME: 20 minutes

MICROWAVE COOKING TIME: 5-6 minutes

MAKES: 12-16 bars

2oz unsweetened chocolate
½ cup butter or margarine
1 cup sugar

1 tsp instant coffee dissolved in 2 tsps hot water
¾ cup all-purpose flour
½ tsp baking powder
2 eggs
Pinch salt
1 cup whole pecans
½ cup chocolate chips

Combine unsweetened chocolate, butter, sugar and dissolved coffee in a mixing bowl. Microwave on MEDIUM for 3-4 minutes or until the chocolate melts and the sugar dissolves. Beat in the eggs and sift in the flour, baking powder and salt. Stir well to blend the mixture. Spread into an 8 inch square dish. Cover the corners of the dish with foil and put the dish on a rack or an inverted saucer. Cook on HIGH for 5 minutes. Sprinkle on the chips and nuts and remove the foil. Cook further 2 minutes. Cool on a flat surface and cut into even squares while slightly warm. Leave to cool completely before removing from the dish.

Sugar Plums

PREPARATION TIME: 25 minutes

MICROWAVE COOKING TIME: 24 minutes plus 1 minute standing time

MAKES: approximately 48 cookies

⅓ cup butter or margarine
¾ cup dark brown sugar
1 egg
2 tbsps brandy
1¼ cups all-purpose flour
2 cups mixed candied fruit, chopped
½ cup raisins
½ cup dates, chopped
1 cup chopped toasted almonds
½ tsp baking soda
Pinch of salt

FROSTING
4 cups powdered sugar
½ cup hot water
Almond, vanilla and peppermint extract
Lemon juice
Food coloring
Colored sugar
Granulated sugar

Beat the brown sugar and the butter together until light and fluffy. Beat in the egg gradually. Stir in the brandy, fruit and almonds. Sift in the flour, baking soda and salt and stir together well. Form into a ball and wrap well. Refrigerate until firm. Shape into ½ inch balls. Place 8 balls in a circle on a sheet of waxed paper on a microwave baking sheet and cook on MEDIUM for 4 minutes per batch. Leave to stand 1 minute and remove to a rack to cool completely. Mix the powdered sugar and water together and divide the mixture into 4 separate bowls. Tint 1 batch pink and flavor with almond, 1 white, flavored with vanilla, 1 yellow, flavored with lemon juice and 1 green, flavored with mint. Coat an equal number of cookies with each of the frostings and sprinkle colored sugar on the top while the frosting is still slightly damp.

Butterscotch Brownies

PREPARATION TIME: 15 minutes

MICROWAVE COOKING TIME: 7 minutes

MAKES: 12-15 bars

½ cup butter or margarine
¾ cup brown sugar
2 eggs
½ tsp vanilla
¾ cup all-purpose flour
½ tsp baking powder
Pinch salt
½ cup raisins
1 cup roughly chopped walnuts
Powdered sugar

Melt the butter for 1 minute on HIGH. Stir in the sugar until well

Facing page: Walnut Fingers (top) and Peanut Butter Thumb Print Cookies (bottom). This page: Sugar Plums.

blended. Beat in the egg. Sift in the flour, baking powder and salt. Stir well and add the raisins. Pour into an 8 inch square dish. Cover the corners of the dish with foil. Place the dish on a rack or on an inverted saucer. Cook for 5 minutes on HIGH. Remove the foil, sprinkle on the nuts and press down lightly. Cook a further 2 minutes on MEDIUM. Cut into bars while still slightly warm. Cool in a dish on a flat surface. Remove from the dish when cool.

CAKES

Jam and Cream Layer Cake

PREPARATION TIME: 25 minutes

MICROWAVE COOKING TIME:
13-21 minutes plus 5 minutes standing time

SERVES: 6-8 people

CAKE
1 cup butter or margarine
1 cup sugar
½ tsp vanilla extract
4 cups all-purpose flour
2 tsps baking powder

FROSTING
2 cups powdered sugar
½ cup hot water
Redcurrant jelly or seedless raspberry jam

FILLING
½ cup whipped cream
4 tbsps strawberry or raspberry jam

Line 2 8 inch cake dishes with 2 layers of wax paper. Beat the butter or margarine to soften. Beat in the sugar until light and fluffy. Beat in the eggs, one at a time, mixing until the mixture is light. Beat in the vanilla and fold in sifted flour and baking powder. Divide the mixture between the 2 dishes and smooth the tops. Bake on highest setting of a combination microwave-convection oven for 12 minutes, or on MEDIUM in a conventional microwave oven for 6 minutes per layer, increasing to HIGH for 2-8 minutes per layer, until done. The cake will look set on the top and the mixture will pull away from the sides of the dish when done. Cool 5-10 minutes on a flat surface before

transferring to a cooling rack to cool completely. Remove the paper from the cakes and choose the layer with the flattest top and spread the other with jam. Spread over the cream and then press on the top layer. Mix the powdered sugar and the water together until of thick coating

This page: Jam and Cream Layer Cake. Facing page: Black Forest Torte.

consistency. Pour the frosting on the top layer and allow to set briefly but not completely. Fill a pastry bag fitted with a small tube with the redcurrant

jelly or raspberry jam. Pipe thin lines of jelly or jam onto the frosting. Draw a knife blade or a skewer back and forth through the frosting and the jelly to feather the lines. This must be done quickly before the frosting sets completely. Allow to set thoroughly before slicing to serve. *Note:* It may be necessary to heat the redcurrant jelly for the feathered lines for 1 minute on HIGH to soften before piping. If the jelly appears full of lumps rub through a fine strainer before using.

Lemon-Glazed Gingerbread

PREPARATION TIME: 20 minutes

MICROWAVE COOKING TIME:
10-13 minutes plus 5-10 minutes standing time

SERVES: 6-8 people

⅓ cup vegetable shortening
⅓ cup light brown sugar
1¼ cups all-purpose flour
Pinch salt
½ tsp baking soda
¼ tsp ground cloves
½ tsp ground cinnamon
½ tsp ground ginger
⅓ cup molasses
¼ cup hot water

GLAZE
¾ cup sugar
1½ tbsps butter or margarine (optional)
Juice and rind of 1 small lemon
¾ cup water

TOPPING
1 cup whipped cream
½ cup sour cream or yogurt
Sugar to taste

Beat the shortening to soften. Beat in the sugar until mixture is light and fluffy. Add the flour, sifted if necessary, salt, soda and spices. Mix the molasses, water and eggs together. Pour into the mixture and beat by hand or machine until just mixed. Spread into an 8 inch round baking dish. Cook on MEDIUM for 6 minutes and then increase the setting to HIGH and cook 1-4 minutes until

set. Cool on a flat surface for 5-10 minutes before transferring to a serving dish. To prepare the glaze, pare the rind from the lemon and scrape off any white pith. Cut the rind into thin slivers and set aside. Combine the remaining ingredients and cook for 2 minutes on HIGH, stirring every 1 minute until the sauce begins to thicken. Add the strips of lemon rind and cook an additional 1 minute on HIGH, stirring once. Do not overcook. The sauce will thicken as it cools. Mix the topping ingredients together. Spoon some of the glaze over the cake, top with the sour cream mixture and pour over the remaining glaze as a sauce.

Pineapple-Apricot Upside-Down Cake

PREPARATION TIME: 25 minutes

MICROWAVE COOKING TIME:
9-15 minutes plus 5-10 minutes standing time

SERVES: 6-8 people

CAKE
⅓ cup butter or margarine
⅔ cup sugar
½ tsp vanilla extract
2 eggs
1 cup all-purpose flour
2 tsps baking powder
¼-⅓ cup milk

TOPPING
1 small fresh pineapple, peeled, cored and sliced or 9 canned pineapple rings
3-4 fresh apricots or 6-8 canned apricot halves
6-8 walnut halves
¼ cup butter or margarine
½ cup light brown sugar

Beat the margarine or butter until soft. Beat in the sugar gradually until the mixture is light and fluffy. Beat in the eggs gradually and add vanilla extract. Stir in the flour and baking powder, sifting if necessary. Add enough of the milk to make the mixture of dropping consistency. Melt the butter or margarine in an

8 inch round dish for 1 minute on HIGH. Sprinkle the sugar evenly over the butter and top with the pineapple rings cut in half and placed in the middle. Around the outside edge place the walnut halves, rounded sides down. Cover each walnut half with an apricot, cut side down. Top with the cake mixture and carefully spread it over the topping. Put the dish on a rack or an inverted saucer and cook 6 minutes on MEDIUM. Increase the setting to HIGH and cook a further 3-8 minutes or until the top appears set. Cool on a flat surface for 5-10 minutes before turning out onto a serving dish. Serve warm with whipped cream.

Passion Cake

PREPARATION TIME: 20 minutes

MICROWAVE COOKING TIME:
14-22 minutes

SERVES: 8-10 people

CAKE
2½ cups all-purpose flour
1¼ cups sugar
8oz carrots, finely grated
8oz canned pineapple, drained and finely chopped
1 tbsp ground cinnamon
2 tsps ground allspice
2 tsps baking powder
4 eggs
⅔ cup butter or margarine
½ cup chopped walnuts

FROSTING
2-8oz packages cream cheese
½ cup powdered sugar
Juice of 1 lemon
Milk

DECORATION
Walnut halves tossed in powdered sugar

Facing page: Lemon-Glazed Gingerbread (top) and Pineapple-Apricot Upside-Down Cake (bottom).

Line 2 9 inch sandwich layer cake dishes with 2 circles of wax paper. Beat the sugar and butter together until light and creamy. Beat in the eggs gradually. Add the carrots, pineapple and walnuts. Sift the flour, baking powder and spices into the mixture and fold in. Divide the mixture between the 2 dishes and bake 1 layer at a time for 6 minutes on MEDIUM per layer. Increase the setting to HIGH and continue to cook for 1-5 minutes more per layer. Cook both layers at a time on the highest setting of a combination microwave-convection oven for 12 minutes. Leave the cakes to stand for 5-10 minutes before turning out to cool on a wire rack. Beat the cheese, sugar and lemon juice together until smooth and spreadable. Add milk, if necessary, until the frosting is of the right consistency. Sandwich the layers together with half the frosting and spread the rest on the top. Decorate with the sugar-coated walnuts around the outside edge of the cake.

Boston Caramel Cream Pie

PREPARATION TIME: 25 minutes

MICROWAVE COOKING TIME: 17½-20 minutes plus 5-10 minutes standing time

SERVES: 6-8 people

CAKE
⅓ cup margarine or butter
⅔ cup sugar
2 eggs
½ tsp vanilla extract
1¼ cups all-purpose flour
2 tsps baking powder
¼-⅓ cup milk

FILLING
¼ cup dark brown sugar
2 tbsps cornstarch
1 cup milk
2 egg yolks
1 tbsp butter or margarine

FROSTING
½ oz unsweetened cooking chocolate

1 cup powdered sugar
¼ cup or more hot water
2 tsps vegetable oil
Note: If using semi-sweet chocolate use
　2 tbsps less powdered sugar

Mix the margarine or butter until soft. Beat in the sugar gradually until the mixture is light and fluffy. Beat in the eggs gradually and add the vanilla extract. Sift in the flour and baking powder and fold in the dry ingredients. Add enough of the milk to make the mixture of dropping consistency. Line the bottom of an 8 inch round dish with 2 layers of wax paper. Cook on MEDIUM for 6 minutes. Increase the setting to HIGH and cook for 2-5 minutes more until the center has risen and the surface appears set. Leave to cool on a flat surface for 5-10 minutes before removing from the baking dish. If using a combination microwave-convection oven use the highest temperature setting and cook for 11 minutes.
Put the sugar for the filling into a deep mixing bowl or glass measure. Heat for 30 seconds on HIGH until melted. Mix the milk into the cornstarch and beat the mixture into the sugar. Cook on HIGH for about 6 minutes, stirring every 2 minutes until very thick. Beat the yolks together and add a spoonful of the hot mixture. Return the eggs to the remaining caramel mixture and blend well. Heat 1 minute on MEDIUM to cook the eggs. Beat in the butter. Put a damp wax paper onto the surface of the filling, and allow to cool slightly. Cut the cake layer in half horizontally and sandwich with the filling.
Melt the chocolate for the frosting for 2 minutes on MEDIUM. Sift in the sugar and stir in enough water to make a thick but pourable frosting. Beat in the oil to keep the frosting shiny. Pour the frosting all at once on top of the cake. Ease the frosting out over the top of the cake with a spatula and allow it to drip down the sides of the cake. Let the frosting set completely before cutting to serve.

Black Forest Torte

PREPARATION TIME: 30 minutes

MICROWAVE COOKING TIME: 26-33 minutes

SERVES: 6-8 people

CAKE
2 squares unsweetened chocolate
1⅓ cups sugar
⅔ cup butter or margarine
4 eggs
1¼ cups all-purpose flour
½ cup cocoa
1 tsp baking soda
¾ cup milk

PASTRY
⅔ cup butter or margarine
¼ cup sugar
½ tsp vanilla extract
1 cup all-purpose flour
1 egg yolk
2 tbsps raspberry jam or redcurrant jelly, melted

FILLING
1-8oz can dark, sweet cherries, pitted
1 tbsp cornstarch
2 tbsps kirsch
½ cup whipped cream, with sugar and kirsch to taste

FROSTING
2 cups whipped cream
Grated chocolate
Maraschino cherries

Mix the butter and sugar together for the pastry until well blended, stir in the egg yolk and vanilla. Stir in the flour until the mixture comes together. Rub well and chill 10 minutes. Roll the pastry out to ¼ inch thick. Prick lightly and cut out into a 9 inch circle. Bake on a microwave baking sheet lined with waxed paper for 5-8 minutes on HIGH. Transfer to a wire rack to cool.
Line 2 8 inch round dishes with 2 layers of wax paper. Melt the chocolate for the cake 4 minutes on

Facing page: Passion Cake (top) and Boston Caramel Cream Pie (bottom)

MEDIUM, stirring once or twice. Allow to cool slightly. Beat the butter or margarine and the sugar together until light. Add the eggs one at a time, beating well between each addition. Fold in the flour, cocoa and baking soda, sifting if necessary. Add the milk and melted chocolate, stirring well to mix, but not overbeating. Spread the butter into the prepared dishes and cook both layers for 12 minutes on the highest temperature in a combination microwave-convection oven or 6 minutes per layer on MEDIUM, increasing to HIGH for 2-5 minutes in a coventional microwave oven. Cool on a flat surface for 5-10 minutes before transferring to a wire rack.

Combine the cherries, juice and cornstarch. Cook on HIGH for 3 minutes, or until thick. Stir in the kirsch and allow to cool. Melt the jam or jelly 1 minute on HIGH, and brush a thin layer over the surface of the pastry. Cut the cake layers in half horizontally. Stick one layer onto the pastry base. Spread on the cherry filling. Sandwich with another cake layer. Top with the kirsch-flavored cream. Top with the cake and cherry filling. End with a cake layer. Cover the top and sides with half of the remaining whipped cream. Sprinkle the grated chocolate on the sides and the top. Pipe a decoration of cream on top of the cake and decorate with the cherries.

Cherry Almond Cakes

PREPARATION TIME: 20 minutes

MICROWAVE COOKING TIME:
6 minutes

MAKES: 6-8 cakes

CAKES
4 eggs
½ cup sugar
1 cup all-purpose flour
¼ cup butter or margarine

FROSTING
¼ cup butter or margarine
2 cups powdered sugar
1 tbsp light cream
1 jar maraschino cherries, juice reserved

DECORATION
Maraschino cherries cut in half
Whole, unblanched almonds

Grease 6-8 custard cups or muffin pans and place a circle of wax paper in the bottom of each cup. Beat the eggs and sugar together until light and fluffy. Heat the butter 2 minutes on LOW to soften. Sift the flour, if necessary, and sprinkle over the surface of the beaten eggs. Pour on the butter and fold into the eggs with the flour. Spoon into the prepared dishes or pans and place on a rack or an inverted saucer. Cook on the highest setting of a combination microwave-convection oven for 5 minutes or on HIGH for 5 minutes in a conventional microwave oven. Leave to stand for 5-10 minutes on a flat surface before turning out onto a wire rack to cool. Reserve 4 cherries and chop the rest. Stir into the frosting with the almonds and kirsch or flavoring. Add more cream if necessary to bring to a smooth spreading consistency. Turn the cakes over so that the base is larger in diameter than the top. Spread over the cherry frosting and top each cake with half a maraschino cherry and 1 blanched almond.

Bombe au Chocolat

PREPARATION TIME: 30 minutes

MICROWAVE COOKING TIME:
5-6 minutes

SERVES: 6-8 people

CAKE
4 eggs
½ cup sugar
1 cup all-purpose flour
¼ cup butter

FROSTING
1oz unsweetened cooking chocolate
¼ cup butter or margarine
⅓ cup milk
4 cups powdered sugar
2 tbsps brandy

DECORATION
Chopped, browned almonds
Maraschino cherries

To prepare the frosting, heat the chocolate, butter and milk for 3-4 minutes on MEDIUM. Stir occasionally until of creamy consistency. Stir in the remaining ingredients. Allow the frosting to cool completely and beat until creamy. Add more milk if necessary. When the cake has cooled split in 4, divide the frosting in half and flavor half with the brandy. Sandwich the layers together starting with the largest flat layer and ending with the small round layer on top. Cover the whole cake with the remaining chocolate frosting and reserve about ⅓ for piping if desired. Pipe on rosettes or ropes of frosting using a fluted tube. Sprinkle over the nuts. Lightly sprinkle with powdered sugar and decorate with the cherries.

Coffee and Lemon Petit Gateaux

PREPARATION TIME: 30 minutes

MICROWAVE COOKING TIME: 9 minutes

MAKES: 16 cakes

4 eggs
½ cup sugar
1 cup all-purpose flour
¼ cup butter or margarine

GLAZE FROSTING
2 cups powdered sugar
½ cup water
Juice of ½ lemon
2 tbsps instant coffee
Few drops yellow food coloring

BUTTERCREAM FROSTING
1 tbsp butter
1 tbsp milk
1 cup powdered sugar
Few drops vanilla extract

APRICOT GLAZE
1 cup apricot jam, sieved
Juice of ½ lemon

Facing page: Bombe au Chocolat. This page: Coffee and Lemon Petit Gateaux (top) and Cherry Almond Cakes (bottom).

Grease a 2 cup round-based mixing bowl with butter and dust lightly with flour. Beat the eggs and sugar until light and fluffy. Heat the butter 2 minutes on LOW to soften. Sift the flour if necessary and sprinkle over the surface of the beaten eggs. Pour on the butter and fold into the egg mixture with the flour. Spread into the prepared bowl and place on a rack or an inverted saucer. Cook on a combination setting in a microwave-convection oven on the highest temperature for 5 minutes, or on HIGH for 5-6 minutes in a conventional microwave oven. Leave to stand for 5-10 minutes before turning out onto a wire rack to cool.

Line an 8 inch square dish with 2 layers of wax paper. Beat the eggs and sugar until thick and mousse-like.

Heat the butter for 2 minutes on LOW to soften. Sift the flour, if necessary, and sprinkle over the surface of the beaten eggs. Pour on the butter and fold into the eggs with the flour. Spread into the prepared dish and place on a rack or an inverted saucer. Cook on the highest setting of a combination microwave-convection oven for 5 minutes or on HIGH in a conventional microwave oven for 5 minutes. Leave to stand for 5-10 minutes on a flat surface before turning out onto a wire rack to cool completely. Cut in desired shapes, rectangles or squares. The cake may also be cut with cookie cutters in rounds or heartshapes, but this will make less than 16 cakes. Cook the jam and lemon juice for 1 minute on HIGH. Brush the cakes on the tops and sides while the glaze is still warm and allow the glaze to set. Divide the powdered sugar in half. Add lemon juice, half the water and yellow food coloring to one half. Beat until smooth. Heat the remaining water until boiling and dissolve the coffee. Add to the remaining sugar and beat until smooth. Pour the lemon frosting over half of the cakes and the coffee frosting over the other half and allow to set completely. Decorate with the buttercream frosting using a small fluted pastry tube and allow to set before serving.

Queen of Sheba

PREPARATION TIME: 25 minutes

MICROWAVE COOKING TIME: 13-20 minutes

SERVES: 6-8 people

⅓ cup butter or margarine
2 squares unsweetened chocolate
¾ cup sugar
3 eggs
1 cup ground almonds
¼ cup all-purpose flour
½ tsp almond extract

GLACÉ FROSTING
2 cups powdered sugar
1 square unsweetened chocolate

¼ cup water
1 tbsp vegetable oil

DECORATION
Blanched, halved almonds
Candied violet or rose petals

Line a 7 inch cake dish with 2 layers of wax paper. Melt the chocolate for 2 minutes on MEDIUM and set aside. Beat the butter or margarine and sugar together until light and creamy. Add the almond extract. Beat in the eggs 1 at a time. Cook on highest setting of a combination microwave-convection oven for 11 minutes, or cook for 12 minutes on MEDIUM increasing to HIGH for 1-6 minutes in a conventional microwave oven. Melt the chocolate for the frosting in the water 2 minutes on MEDIUM. Pour into the powdered sugar and beat until smooth. Add the oil to keep the frosting shiny and more water if necessary to bring to thick coating consistency. Pour over the cake all at once and ease down the sides with a spatula to cover completely. Allow to set slightly before arranging the decoration. Allow to set completely before slicing to serve.
Note: If using semi-sweet chocolate in the cake and frosting recipe omit 2 tbsps of the required sugar for each.

Devil's Food Cake with Seafoam Frosting

PREPARATION TIME: 25 minutes

MICROWAVE COOKING TIME: 25-29 minutes

SERVES: 6-8 people

2 squares unsweetened chocolate
⅔ cup butter or margarine
1⅓ cups sugar
4 eggs
1¾ cups all-purpose flour
½ cup cocoa
1 tsp baking soda
¾ cup milk

FROSTING
2 cups sugar

⅔ cup water
Small pinch cream of tartar
4 egg whites
1 tsp vanilla extract
3oz semi-sweet chocolate

Line 2 8 inch round dishes with 2 layers of wax paper. Melt the chocolate for the cake for 1 minute on MEDIUM, stirring once or twice. Allow to cool slightly. Meanwhile, beat the butter or margarine and sugar together until light. Add the eggs one at a time, beating well between each addition. Fold in the flour, baking soda and cocoa, sifting if necessary. Add milk and chocolate, stirring to mix well but not overbeating. Spread the batter into the prepared dishes. Cook both layers for 12 minutes on the highest temperature in a combination microwave-convection oven, or 6 minutes per layer on MEDIUM increasing to HIGH for 2-5 minutes in a conventional microwave oven. Cool on a flat surface for 5-10 minutes before turning out onto a wire rack to cool completely. To prepare the frosting combine the water and sugar in a deep bowl. Cook to a syrup, stirring frequently. The syrup should register 240°F/ 130°C on a sugar thermometer. Beat the egg whites with the cream of tartar until stiff peaks form. Gradually beat in the sugar syrup until the frosting is stiff and glossy. If the frosting will not stiffen beat in up to 2 cups powdered sugar. Add vanilla extract. Sandwich the layers with the frosting, reserving enough for the top and sides. Swirl the frosting on the top and sides and melt the chocolate on MEDIUM for 2 minutes. Drizzle the chocolate on top of the cake and allow it to drip down the sides. Allow the frosting and the chocolate to set before slicing to serve.

Facing page: Devil's Food Cake with Seafoam Frosting (top) and Queen of Sheba (bottom).

DESSERTS & CONFECTIONERY

Danish Fruit Shortcake

PREPARATION TIME: 25 minutes

MICROWAVE COOKING TIME:
9 minutes plus 1 hour minimum
standing time

SERVES: 6-8 people

½ cup powdered sugar
2 cups all-purpose flour
⅔ cup butter or margarine
½ tsp vanilla extract
1 egg
1lb strawberries
1 cup redcurrant jelly or seedless raspberry
    jam
1 cup whipped cream
Mint leaves

Work the flour and sugar briefly in a
food processor to sift. Add the
butter, cut into small pieces and add
vanilla extract. Work until the
mixture resembles fine breadcrumbs.
Add the egg and work until the
mixture comes together. If the
mixture is too soft at this point chill
for 15-20 minutes. Line a large glass
pie dish or flan dish or a large baking
sheet with wax paper. Press out the
dough into an 8-9 inch round. Crimp
the edges and chill for 15 minutes.
Cook 8 minutes on LOW. Leave to
cool on a baking sheet or in the dish
for 1 hour or more before removing.
Pastry may also be cooked in a
combination microwave-convection
oven for 8 minutes on a moderate
temperature setting. Lift the pastry
carefully onto a serving dish. If the
strawberries are small leave them
whole, otherwise cut in half
lengthwise. Heat the jelly or jam in a
jar or deep bowl for 1 minute on
HIGH, stirring once, to help soften.
Brush the pastry with the hot glaze

**This page: Chocolate Orange
Cheesecake. Facing page: Danish
Fruit Shortcake.**

and leave to set for a minute.
Arrange the strawberries, cut side
down if sliced. Brush with the hot
glaze and leave to cool and set. Whip
the cream and pipe rosettes around
the edge of the strawberries and
decorate each rosette with a mint leaf
before serving.

*Chocolate Orange
Cheesecake*

PREPARATION TIME: 25 minutes

MICROWAVE COOKING TIME:
15 minutes

SERVES: 8-10 people

CRUST
¼ cup butter
1½ cups crushed chocolate cookies

FILLING
2oz semi-sweet chocolate
2 tbsps water

remaining chocolate and water for 30 seconds to 1 minute on MEDIUM, stirring until smooth. Drizzle over the oranges. Allow the chocolate to set before serving.

Hazelnut Meringues with Black Cherry Sauce

PREPARATION TIME: 20 minutes

MICROWAVE COOKING TIME: 6 minutes

SERVES: 8-10 people

MERINGUES
1 egg white
2½ cups powdered sugar
¼ cup finely chopped, browned hazelnuts
2 cups whipped cream

SAUCE
8oz can dark sweet cherries, pitted
2 tbsps cornstarch
1 tbsp kirsch or cherry brandy

DECORATION
Cocoa powder

Beat the egg white lightly and add the powdered sugar and hazelnuts. Stir to form a pliable dough. Roll the dough into a thin sausage about ½ inch thick. Cut into small pieces and place well apart on wax paper on a microwave baking sheet. Flatten the pieces slightly. Cook for 1 minute on HIGH until dry. The meringues will triple in size. Leave to cool on a wire rack. Combine the cornstarch and cherries. Cook 5 minutes on HIGH stirring once after 2 minutes. When thickened, add the kirsch or cherry brandy and set aside. Cut a long strip of wax paper about 1 inch wide, line up half the meringues and lay the strip across them. Sprinkle cocoa powder on the exposed ends of both sides of the meringues. Spread the undecorated meringue with whipped cream and place the decorated meringues on top. Serve with the cherry sauce.

2 8oz packages cream cheese
⅔ cup sugar
⅓ cup plain yogurt
Grated rind and juice of 1 orange
4 eggs

TOPPING
2 oranges, peeled and segmented
1oz semi-sweet chocolate
1 tbsp water

Melt the butter for the crust 1 minute on HIGH. Crush the cookies in a food processor and add the butter. Place the crust onto a base of an 8 inch dish with a removable base, if possible. Cook the crust for 1 minute on HIGH. Melt the chocolate for the filling with the water for 30 seconds on MEDIUM, stirring occasionally.

This page: Hazelnut Meringues with Black Cherry Sauce. Facing page: Chocolate Brandy Cake.

Mix the remaining ingredients for the filling until smooth. Cook for 4 minutes on HIGH, stirring well every 2 minutes. Pour ⅓ of the filling onto the crust base. Drizzle ⅓ of the chocolate onto the filling and carefully marble it through using a skewer or a knife. Do not disturb the base. Repeat until all the filling and chocolate is used. Cook an additional 10 minutes on MEDIUM or until softly set in the centre. Chill until firm. Remove the cake to a serving dish and arrange the orange segments around the edge of the cake. Mix the

Chocolate Brandy Cake

PREPARATION TIME: 20 minutes plus chilling overnight

MICROWAVE COOKING TIME: 7 minutes

SERVES: 8 people

12oz semi-sweet chocolate
½ cup butter
¼ cup brandy
2 eggs
2 cups graham crackers, coarsely crushed
½ cup chopped almonds
1 cup whipped cream
Candied violet or rose petals
Toasted almonds
Slivers of angelica

Melt the chocolate and butter together on MEDIUM for 5 minutes. Beat in the eggs and heat a further 2 minutes on MEDIUM stirring twice to thicken the eggs. Stir in the brandy, crackers and chopped almonds. Spread into a 7 inch springform or removable base pan. Chill overnight until firm. Transfer to a serving dish and decorate with rosettes of cream, almonds, angelica and candied violet or rose petals.

Lemon Ginger Pudding Cake

PREPARATION TIME: 20 minutes

MICROWAVE COOKING TIME: 12 minutes

SERVES: 6 people

¾ cup white sugar
1 cup all-purpose flour
2 tsps baking powder
2 tbsps butter
Grated rind and juice of 1 lemon
2 pieces preserved or crystallised ginger, chopped
½ cup milk
1 cup brown sugar
1½ cups cold water

Sift the flour if necessary and combine with ¾ cup white sugar and baking powder. Melt the butter for 1 minute on HIGH and combine with the milk, lemon juice and rind and ginger. Beat the liquid ingredients into the dry ingredients and spoon into a 9 inch round baking dish. Scatter the brown sugar over the top and pour over the cold water. Cook on MEDIUM for 10 minutes and 2 minutes on HIGH, or 12 minutes on a combination setting in a microwave-convection oven. Pudding will separate into a cake layer on top and a sauce underneath. Do not allow the pudding to overcook. Serve warm or chilled with whipped cream.

Chocolate Flans

PREPARATION TIME: 20 minutes

MICROWAVE COOKING TIME: 24-25 minutes

SERVES: 6-8 people

CARAMEL
½ cup water
½ cup granulated sugar

CUSTARD
3 eggs
2oz semi-sweet chocolate
1½ cups milk
1 cinnamon stick

DECORATION
6-8 pecan halves
Chocolate curls

Put water and sugar for the caramel into a deep bowl or glass measure. Stir well. Cook on HIGH for 12 minutes until golden. Stir once or twice at the beginning of cooking to help dissolve the sugar. Do not overcook the caramel; it will continue to darken after it is removed from the oven. Pour the caramel quickly into 6-8 custard cups that have been warmed briefly in the oven. Leave the caramel to cool and harden. Melt the chocolate in the milk for 5 minutes on HIGH with the cinnamon. Beat the egg and strain on the milk, blending well. Discard the cinnamon stick. Pour onto the hardened caramel in each dish. Put the dishes into a shallow dish in a circle with enough hot water to come halfway up the sides. Cook on LOW for 7-8 minutes or until set. Chill completely and turn out onto serving plates. Decorate with chocolate curls and pecans.

Chocolate Almond Pudding Cake

PREPARATION TIME: 20 minutes

MICROWAVE COOKING TIME: 12 minutes

SERVES: 6 people

¾ cup sugar
1 cup all-purpose flour
2 tsps baking powder
2 tbsps butter
3 tbsps cocoa
½ cup milk
½ tsp almond extract
½ cup chopped almonds
½ cup brown sugar
½ cup sugar
4 tbsps cocoa
1½ cups cold water

Sift the flour if necessary and combine with ¾ cup sugar. Melt butter 1 minute on HIGH and combine with 3 tbsps cocoa, almond extract and milk. Beat the liquid ingredients into the dry ingredients and fold in the nuts. Spoon into a 9 inch round baking dish. Scatter the brown sugar, remaining white sugar and cocoa over the top without mixing. Pour over the water and bake on MEDIUM for 10 minutes and 2 minutes on HIGH, or 12 minutes on a combination setting of a microwave-convection oven. The pudding will separate into a cake layer on top and a sauce underneath. Do not overbake. Serve with whipped cream if desired.

Facing page: Lemon Ginger Pudding Cake (top) and Chocolate Almond Pudding Cake (bottom).

Cherry Nut Balls

PREPARATION TIME: 20 minutes

MICROWAVE COOKING TIME:
10-13 minutes

MAKES: about 16 balls

2 cups candied cherries
¾ cup sugar
½ cup butter or margarine
2 cups crisp rice cereal, crushed
½ cup chopped walnuts
1 egg
2 tbsps evaporated milk
Desiccated coconut

Combine butter and sugar in a medium bowl. Cook for 4 minutes on HIGH. Chop the cherries finely and add to the bowl. Stir well and cook 1 minute further on HIGH. Mix the egg and the milk. Add gradually to the hot cherry mixture, stirring well. Cook on MEDIUM for 5-8 minutes or until the mixture comes together in a ball when stirred. Mix in the cereal and nuts, and shape into 1 inch balls. Roll in desiccated coconut and allow to set before serving. Cherry nut balls keep 2 weeks in an airtight container.

White Coffee Creams

PREPARATION TIME: 20 minutes

MICROWAVE COOKING TIME:
10-11 minutes plus 30 minutes standing time

SERVES: 6-8 people

1 cup milk
8 coffee beans
3 eggs
¼ cup sugar
½ cup light cream

SAUCE
2 cups blackberries, blackcurrants or
*   raspberries*
1 tbsp lemon juice
Powdered sugar to taste
Water

**This page: Cherry Nut Balls (top)
and Chocolate Truffles (bottom).
Facing page: Chocolate Flans (top)
and White Coffee Creams (bottom).**

Chocolate Truffles

PREPARATION TIME: 20 minutes

MICROWAVE COOKING TIME:
4½ minutes

MAKES: 30 balls

6oz chocolate chips
2 tsps instant coffee or brandy
2 tsps light cream
2 egg yolks
1 tbsp butter

COATING
Cocoa
Ground blanched almonds

Melt the chocolate with the coffee, if using, for 4½ minutes on MEDIUM. Add the remaining ingredients and beat well until thick and cool. If using brandy, add with the rest of the ingredients. Chill until firm. Roll into 1 inch balls. Roll half in the cocoa and half in the ground, blanched almonds.

DECORATION
Whole berries
Mint leaves

Put the coffee beans and milk into a small, deep bowl. Heat 3 minutes on HIGH. Set aside 30 minutes to infuse. Beat the egg and the sugar together until thick. Strain on the milk and add the cream. Pour into 6-8 custard cups. Put into a shallow dish in a circle with enough hot water to come halfway up the sides of the dishes. Cook on LOW for 7-8 minutes or until set. Chill completely. Combine berries, juice and sugar in a blender or food processor, reserving 6-8 for decoration. Process until the berries break down. If the sauce is too thick add water to thin slightly. Strain to remove the seeds. Loosen the creams from the sides of the dishes and turn out onto individual plates. Pour round the sauce and decorate with the berries and mint leaves.

Rocky Road Fudge

PREPARATION TIME: 20 minutes
MICROWAVE COOKING TIME: 20 minutes
MAKES: 1lb

2 cups sugar
¾ cup milk
2oz unsweetened chocolate
¼ cup butter or margarine
2 tsps vanilla extract
1 cup miniature marshmallows
½ cup coarsely chopped walnuts

Put the sugar and milk into a large bowl. Add the chocolate, finely chopped, and butter. Cover the bowl with pierced plastic wrap and cook on HIGH for 5 minutes or until boiling. Stir well and cook a further 15 minutes, uncovered, on MEDIUM. Stir frequently. The mixture should form a soft ball when a small amount is dropped into cold water. Leave to cool until barely warm. Beat in the vanilla extract and continue beating until the mixture thickens and starts to lose its shine.

Quickly add the nuts and marshmallows and spread into an 8 inch square dish lined with wax paper. Mark into squares and leave to set before removing from the dish.

Coffee Raspberry Roulades

PREPARATION TIME: 25 minutes
MICROWAVE COOKING TIME: 3 minutes per batch
SERVES: 6-8 people

1 tbsp butter
6 egg whites
1½ cups sugar
2 tsps cornstarch
1 tsp cream of tartar
1 tsp vinegar
2 tsps instant coffee dissolved in 1 tsp boiled water
½ cup toasted, sliced almonds

FILLING
1 cup whipped cream
2 cups raspberries, fresh or frozen

DECORATION
Powdered sugar
Coffee bean dragées

Melt the butter for 30 seconds on HIGH. Line several baking sheets with wax paper and brush the paper with the melted butter. Beat egg whites until stiff but not dry. Beat in the sugar a spoonful at a time, beating well in between each addition. Mix the vinegar with the coffee and fold into egg whites with the cornstarch and cream of tartar. Divide the mixture into 12 equal portions. Smooth each portion out into a rectangle about ½ inch thick on the baking sheets. Sprinkle on the almonds and cook for 3 minutes on HIGH per batch and leave to cool slightly. Sprinkle a sheet of wax paper or a clean towel with powdered sugar and turn the roulades over almond side down. Whip the cream and spread half of it over the rolls and scatter on the raspberries, reserving 12 for garnish. Roll up each roulade, from long end to long end as for a jelly roll. Pipe the remaining cream

on top using a rosette pastry tube. Decorate with coffee bean dragées and remaining raspberries to serve.

Honeycomb

PREPARATION TIME: 20 minutes
MICROWAVE COOKING TIME: 10-16 minutes
MAKES: approximately 1lb

1 cup sugar
1 cup light corn syrup
1 tbsp white or wine vinegar
1 tbsp baking soda

COATING
8oz semi-sweet or milk chocolate

Line an 8 inch square dish with oiled foil. Combine sugar, syrup and vinegar in a large, deep bowl, cover with pierced plastic wrap and cook on HIGH for 3 minutes, stirring frequently to dissolve the sugar. Uncover and cook a further 4-10 minutes on HIGH, or until the mixture reaches 300°F/150°C on a sugar thermometer or until a small amount of the mixture forms brittle threads when dropped in cold water. Quickly add the soda to the mixture and stir it well. The mixture will foam when the soda is added. Pour into the prepared dish and leave until firm. Remove from the dish and break into pieces about 2 inch. The pieces will be irregular in shape. Melt the chocolate for 3 minutes on MEDIUM in a deep bowl. Coat half of the honeycomb with the chocolate and allow it to set before serving. The remaining honeycomb may be served plain.

Facing page: Honeycomb (top) and Rocky Road Fudge (bottom).

Steamed Chocolate-Fig Pudding

PREPARATION TIME: 20 minutes

MICROWAVE COOKING TIME: 7-9 minutes plus 5-10 minutes standing time

SERVES: 6-8 people

⅓ cup butter or margarine
1 cup sugar
2 eggs
1½ cups all-purpose flour
2 tbsps cocoa powder
1 tsp baking soda
1 tbsp brandy
1 cup water
1 cup semi-sweet chocolate chips
1½ cups dried figs, chopped
1 cup toasted hazelnuts, chopped

Grease a 4 cup mixing bowl or decorative mold very well with butter or margarine. Beat the remaining butter and sugar until light and fluffy. Beat in the eggs one at a time. Add the flour, unsifted, cocoa and baking soda. Add the brandy, water, figs, almonds and chocolate chips. Pour into the prepared dish or mold. Cover with 2 layers of pierced plastic wrap to release the steam. Cook 7-9 minutes on HIGH. Leave to stand 5-10 minutes before serving. Serve with hard sauce or whipped cream.

Steamed Raspberry Jam Pudding

PREPARATION TIME: 20 minutes

MICROWAVE COOKING TIME: 6-8 minutes plus 5-10 minutes standing time

SERVES: 6 people

½ cup raspberry jam
½ cup butter or margarine
½ cup sugar
2 eggs
1 tsp vanilla extract
1 cup all-purpose flour
1 tsp baking powder
2 tbsps milk

Grease a 3 cup mixing bowl or decorative mold very well with butter or margarine. Put the jam into the bottom. Cream the remaining butter or margarine and sugar until light and fluffy. Beat in the eggs one at a time. Add the vanilla, sift in the flour and baking powder and fold in. If the mixture is very stiff add up to 2 tbsps milk to bring to a soft dropping consistency. Spoon the mixture on top of the jam. Cover the top of the bowl or mold with 2 layers of plastic wrap pierced several times to release steam. Cook 6-8 minutes on HIGH. Leave to stand 5-10 minutes before turning out to serve. Serve with whipped cream or custard sauce.

This page: Coffee Raspberry Roulades. Facing page: Steamed Raspberry Jam Pudding (top) and Steamed Chocolate-Fig Pudding (bottom).

INDEX